GW01218030

# Evaporated Children

Written and compiled by Sheila Rowe

To Joan and Ken
With best wishes
from
Sheila Rowe
28th April 2008

Second edition, published in April 2006
The Plynlimmon Press
First edition published in December 2005
The Plynlimmon Press

Copyright Sheila Rowe

0-9552222-0-6
ISBN
978-0-9552222-0-7

Email: john@joots.demon.co.uk

Sheila Rowe has asserted her right to be identified as the author of this work. No part of this publication may be produced, transmitted or stored in a retrieval system in any form or by any means without written permission of the publishers.

A catalogue record of the first edition of this book is available from the British Library.

Printed in Great Britain by
Contact Reprographics
Layer de la Haye
Colchester
Essex
email: norfolk654@aol.com

By the same author:

A Breach of Nature Observed – *Children in War, May 2004, Vol 1, No.1.*
Published by DSM Technical Publications, Peterborough, Cambs.

This book is dedicated to my mother Ethel Rose Jones.

# Acknowledgements

These are the stories of a small group of children all evacuated from the coastal town of Hastings on the same day 21$^{st}$ July 1940 following the evacuation of Dunkirk, when it was feared that Hitler would cross the channel to invade Britain.

Acknowledgements and gratitude are due to all those whose stories are recorded here for their co-operation in allowing me to tape their histories and giving me permission to reproduce them. Many have sent photographs to enhance the text. All have made a huge emotional commitment and remained enthusiastic about having their stories told and been patient with me during the time it took for the telling. Sadly four of them have died since the recordings and I wish to thank two of their widows for giving me permission to publish, Joan – Tony Pelling's wife and Betty – Roy Judge's wife.

**Contributors**; those who wish to remain anonymous are recorded by a pseudonym and some requested Christian names only to be used.

Paddy Bane (nee Dennett)

Jean White (nee Dennett)

Jean Scrivenner

Keith (pseudonym)

Sylvia (pseudonym)

John Farmer (pseudonym)

Peggy Howe (nee Brasier)

Roy Judge

Pricilla (pseudonym) (nee P Buesdon)

Ellen (Eileen Forsyth nee Toogood)

Ned (Norman Toogood )

Margaret

Terry Breeds

Lillian and Daphne

Tony Pelling

"They put us on a train.... Of course it was all a game to us. There were a few cynical members of the party who said that it wasn't a game at all, that it was because of the war... but mum and dad would have told us if it was true. We had survived the shock of war being declared in spite of my father's assurances and our faith was still strong. We weren't to know that this day would end in betrayal,"

Michael Aspel. (*Johson B S. 1968. The Evacuees.* Victor Gollanz Ltd. London).

# I remember the train

Chuffer, chuff, chuff went the train,
I remember the train.
But well before that,
I remember the priest
And my sweet pussy-cat.
The priest had us all in church one day
And said some prayers about going away.
My mother cried hard and hugged me tight
As we wandered home for our last 'good-night'.
Then early next day we were put on a bus
And all said 'good-bye' with a great deal of fuss.
We children queued and our parents stood back
As we climbed the bus steps with our label and pack,
Their arms stretched out in a frantic wave,
With longing and love, some weeping, some brave.
I called "Take care of my sweet pussy cat."
My mum gave the teacher my teddy and hat.
Grandpa said "Let her go, don't fret!"
Not knowing what we were in for yet.
As we left on that bus to go to the train,
We watched as our parents went silent with pain.
Once on the train we soon built up steam,
We chatted and giggled but all in a dream.
People waved as we chuffered and sped by their door,
They knew we'd be seeing our mummies no more.
No one told us how long our journey would be
Or the place where we sped to our destiny.
Chuffer, chuff, chuff went the train.

## Introduction

The voices of these children record a dark period of history; born to parents affected in a deeply emotional way by World War 1 and economically by the depression that followed the 'slump' of the 1920's and 30's. Some saw a way out of poverty for their children through obtaining a place at a fee paying Grammar School by passing the scholarship, which eventually became officially the Eleven Plus Examination after the 1944 Education Act.

World War 11 cast the longest shadow of all as towns and cities came under the threat of bombing or invasion, resulting in all the schools being evacuated. Parents faced the agonizing decision of parting with their children or keeping them at home in an unsafe place and depriving them of any means of education. Much class levelling took place when the children went away, some of the poorest going to stately English homes and some of the more prosperous to existence on a 'shoe string'. Any compensation derived from this was often outbalanced by the pain of separation from their families and trauma imposed by the war itself. All of these children came from the same town Hastings in East Sussex and all left home on the same day, 21st July 1940. Sadly their return was not so well organised, as we shall see. A paternalistic church imposed a strict moral code on many of them; an almost sadistic school discipline kept the boys in order and the emotional life of all was controlled by the need to maintain a stiff upper lip.

In the first chapter, nine year old Paddy, provides the title and gives us a gentle start as she retains her sense of security by having the luck to remain with her sister and being reunited with her mother. Her sister Jean going through the same experiences reveals her own perceptions of them. Jean Scrivener has the advantage of a wealthier life style but this cannot protect her from all the vicissitudes of war. As we move on through the stories we are put in touch with the deeper feelings created by the 'cold' receptions experienced by Keith and a sense of betrayal, abandonment and disillusion expressed by his sister. John reveals the cruelty of the school discipline but the academic Roy finds a means of escape of his own making. Peggy is traumatised by enemy action and the responsibility of feeling responsible for a younger sibling. Pricilla shows us that some reception areas were not safe from bombing. Ellen accepts her 'lot' and is able to survive by denying her foster mother's total rejection and her brother conforms to all requirements until he goes into a state of rebellion to find it doesn't work for him. Margaret and Sylvia show us that child abuse is not a new concept but Terry feels that fortune has smiled on him and revels in his new life. Lilian shows how the dramatic effect of her father becoming a casualty of war affects the whole family and Tony takes us through the ending of the saga: as the evacuees languish away from home there are many others who have to come first. All of these children are old ladies and gentlemen now and it is time to tell their stories before they die with them. They were recorded between 1999 and 2001 and permission obtained from all to publish. Some of the protagonists have provided photographs, some sadly epitaphs but all have bequeathed intense emotional recall and a richness of minutiae that brings to life the meaning of their poverty, educational opportunity, war trauma, the deep sadness of early separation from the people and the places that they loved in Hastings and the problems wrought by time affecting them all as they returned. As we step into this river of time with them; let us ask ourselves these questions. How did their experiences affect the next generation? Do they still carry the burden of their own and their parents' suffering into their old age?

# Contents                                                    Page

# Chapter 1. 'We were going to be evaporated.'

## Paddy Bane's Story.

I was evacuated from Hastings on the 21<sup>st</sup> July 1940 when I was nine years old and my sister was fourteen. We lived at home with just my mother because my father had died the year before which meant we'd had to move to a smaller house. Yes, it was only 1938 when he died and I can't really remember him a lot, I was only seven. We used to live in a big three storied house but my mother had a rough time after my father died and she couldn't afford to stay there so we moved into this little terraced house. She must have soldiered on well because it was a big change for her but she never made us feel it was terrible. When we heard we were going to be evacuated we were quite excited, we were telling everybody we were going to be "evaporated", which we thought was a big joke. I can't remember very much about the journey when we eventually went, except that we went straight through from Hastings to Ware, without changing trains and I've never been able to work out how they did it because you usually have to change in London. When we got there my sister and I were eventually taken to a billet, and the first thing they asked us was whether we had known each other before the war, because we didn't look a bit alike and they didn't realise we were sisters, which we thought was  quite funny. That night my sister was in tears and I said to her, "What's the matter, don't you like it here?" She can't actually remember that but I can.

Our first billet was an enormous house in its own grounds, it seemed like miles outside the town with a big staff and a nursery for the children. There were three children in the family and a nurse to look after them and we ate with them in the nursery. This family was a bit put out because the butler had been called up and they felt hard done by. The first morning we were there we got up and made our own beds and then we were told we needn't make the beds because the maids would do it and if we wanted our shoes cleaned to leave them outside the door at night and they were back in the morning. It was all a bit new to us after coming from a small terraced house in Hastings; but we liked it there because they had this huge garden and I learned to ride a bike because we were allowed to play on theirs and I'd never had one before. The mother of the family was in hospital with tuberculosis and eventually they were going to bring her home. They said she'd have to have complete peace, so the evacuees had to go - which I think was a good excuse to get rid of us. I don't think they really wanted us there in the first place and it was a good excuse to get shot of us because she'd got to have peace and quiet.

From there we went to live in a little house practically in the yard of a factory, by the railway sidings, and the man we were billeted on was the foreman. We never discovered quite what they were making; it was all a secret, something to do with the war. It was totally different from the other place. Every night we used to go down a little 'dug-out' with all the men who were on fire-watch duty, that was quite an adventure because there were a lot of air raids but not many bombs were dropped. My mother got worried about us being there because our foster parents didn't come home until fairly late in the evening, after dark, and she didn't like us being on our own in case there was an air raid. Somehow she managed to get in touch with the authorities and we were found another billet where people were there in the evening to keep an eye on us. So we started off with the gentry and then went downhill with a bump. At this next place we were rather cold in bed and we had awful old coats on the bed instead of blankets. We've always joked about it ever since, my sister and I; if it's cold we always say "Awful old coats". She'll probably tell you the same.
At this place too we used to go down the shelter every night while the air raids were on, they used the school shelters, which were just down the road. It's funny the things you remember. One of the firemen down in the dug-out one night fell down the steps and hit his head on the wall and jammed his tin hat over his ears and he couldn't get it off, everybody was falling about in hysterics, it's things like that you remember, the funny things. Another one of them was called Pussy, because his mother used to have umpteen cats, and when he was a kid they followed him to school and he'd been Pussy all his life apparently, it's the silly things like that that stick in your mind. There are other things that I know happened and I can't remember them at all, they're the things that are not so funny. We did have a few bombs in Ware but not an awful lot. Aircraft came over if they were lost or driven out of London by gunfire and they used to stooge about overhead a lot and we'd be down the dug-out listening to them, it was very noisy because the guns would all be firing. At 1 o'clock in the morning, if the All Clear went, my sister would wake me up and say, "I'm not stopping down here any longer, come on, let's go home to bed" and we'd just say to the others, "We're going

home now" and we'd walk up the road all on our own in the blackout and go in and get into our own beds. The rest of the family would let us go they didn't seem to worry about us but would stay down in the shelter themselves until the morning; but we survived. I don't think my mother knew about that, or that the billet wasn't very clean.

We had to share the same towel with all the family, which wasn't very pleasant, and my sister and I used to have to bath in the water that my foster mother had boiled the towels in. Anyway after a time we both got measles and, probably because of the grubby conditions, I got impetigo and my sister got pneumonia and pleurisy on top of the measles and ended up in hospital. By that time my mother had become so worried she evacuated herself and was living in the town as well, but it was a struggle for her to find somewhere to live, and she had to live in a separate billet because everywhere was full up. She was very concerned because she couldn't look after us and we were both so poorly. I guess my mum had always done everything that she could to hold it all together. Before she came up she used to write to us every week and send us a sixpenny Postal Order each, which we cashed at the Post Office, it was the big event of our week  It seems strange now that I can't remember meeting her when she came to live in Ware and it was the first time I'd seen her for seven months. It was lovely to see my mum again because we hadn't been home for any of the holidays like some girls but I just can't remember her arrival, I can't remember it at all.

I don't know who found this first billet for her but it must have been very worrying for her to be in another place. She would come round to see how we were and was a bit concerned that we weren't getting the right sort of food. She managed to get some new laid eggs sometimes and wrote our names on them to make sure we would have them; she didn't know that our entire egg ration was given to the small boy of the household and we never got an egg at all. He was about five and the apple of everybody's eye, so all the best things went to him. After a while she found an ordinary little house with two bedrooms. A family with a baby lived downstairs, they had the front room and the dining room and used the front room as their bedroom, we had the upstairs and sort of made one of the bedrooms into a living room. We shared their kitchen and everyone shared the bathroom. I suppose it wasn't the best arrangement, it was probably much worse for the two women than it was for the rest of us, kids don't worry so much about sharing things like kitchens. Anyway my mother was working all day and didn't get in the other woman's way.

At that time there were two ladies doing the job of billeting officer as volunteers. They used to drive around in a car and then they decided it was big enough for a full time paid job and they advertised for someone and my mother got the job but she had to do it on her own and walk everywhere because she couldn't drive. She used to be literally walking the streets until 10 o'clock at night sometimes trying to fit people in when there was a big influx of evacuees. She'd stay out until she found somewhere for them all to go and it was very worrying for her at times. It was a marvellous job really because she was working in the Council Offices with the Town Clerk and everybody at Ware who was anybody. In the grounds of the Council Offices there was a little lodge place where the Air Raid Wardens used to work. It was the place where they received coded messages in colour, amber, green or red when there was going to be an air raid and when it showed red they had to sound the sirens, so there would have to be people on duty in there all the evening and sometimes she'd have a game of crib with the men on the quiet because she loved cards, so she'd pop in there at night sometimes just for a game.

Paddy's mother with Ware Town Council members.

After we'd been there some time she managed to get a whole house somewhere else as the old lady who owned it had gone to live with her daughter. My mother rented the house furnished from her and we moved in there. It was a bit dilapidated, it didn't have any electricity but it did have gas lighting, so we weren't too badly off and we had an accumulator battery for our radio, which needed charging every so often. We were without our own things, it was all other people's things in the house but we were quite comfortable after what we'd been through and we stayed there for the rest of the time we were evacuated, four years altogether I think. I made a lot of friends with the local children and always seemed to have plenty to play with and joined in everything but one day, after I'd had an argument with her kid, the woman who lived next door came roaring out and told me that I was lucky to be allowed to play with her children because I was only an evacuee, making me feel like some sort of second class citizen. Yes, I'll always remember that.

It didn't stop me being happy there I did make lots of friends in spite of being an evacuee, mostly boys, but there I was always a tomboy. My sister and I used to go swimming a lot in the little outdoor swimming pool; my mother bought us a season ticket each every summer for the princely sum of six shillings and sixpence, which was an awful lot of money to her, but she knew we'd be all right and she knew where we were. As long as the weather was nice I used to be there all day in the summer. We'd pack up some sandwiches and take them to the little gardens there. When we weren't in the water we would spend a lot of time lying in the sun. I think I remained unscarred from my evacuation because I was able to make some fun there. Another adventure I had was to go round in a little pony and trap collecting pig food for a smallholding near where we lived. The boy I used to go with was a bit older than me but my mother never knew anything about it. Everybody used to save all their scraps in those days in a separate bin for the pigs and I used to go round and help him and when we got back to the smallholding I could have a ride on the pony.

I was at the High School all the time we were away. We had lessons in two church halls and a church, and we had the school in the afternoon when the Ware Grammar School girls had gone home. It didn't worry me very much, I'm afraid I was never very academically minded anyway, so I just did what I had to do. I know while we were away we had to write an essay on the subject of 'How to Find the Way From Hastings Station to My Home' and I couldn't remember - couldn't remember at all, so I said, "I don't know". They looked at me as if I was balmy but I couldn't do it, so I had to write an essay on something else.

So I guess I'm saying Ware became quite important to me in a way, the fact that I'd got established there. I came to like it there very much and eventually, when the whole school moved back, we were left there because my mother was still working, so I was transferred to Ware Grammar School for a time which I liked very much. I liked the staff and I was getting on well and then my mother decided to take us back to Hastings. I said to her, "Can't I stay here and go into lodgings" but she didn't think much of that idea so we all came back. I felt very strange when I moved back to Hastings, I couldn't remember it at all, and it was rather weird. I felt much stranger than when I went to Ware in the first place because I could hardly remember Hastings. I felt really peculiar when I first went back to the school but you sort of adapt and I settled in again I suppose.

Luckily we all came through the war unscathed and we all came home. I can remember the journey home very well because I brought a box of white mice with me. We went in the News Theatre at Victoria Station to wait for the train and I let these mice out and they were running up and down the cinema and my mother nearly had a fit; that was just the sort of thing I did. I was nine when I went away and thirteen when I came back like a stranger and it did feel funny because I felt more of a stranger in Hastings my home than I did in Ware. It may have been the age thing perhaps because I had sort of grown up a lot there and I hadn't been allowed out on my own in Hastings before I left so I didn't know my way around.

I know I was very lucky not to be in a really terrible place and I never had any awful experiences, so I don't think it's affected me. No I can't think of any way that it has. I think children who had terrible experiences probably have been affected and I don't know about my sister who was older than me. She went to work while she was there, she got a job there when she left school, we just sort of fitted in somehow, we adapted. Well you had to didn't you? You had no choice somehow. I had quite a rough ride at the beginning with all those changes but my sister stayed with me all the time and eventually came back with me. So we all kept together, we were lucky you see and I think probably that made a difference. There was somebody to cling to, she was five years older than me and kept an eye on me and my mother helped us retain the family structure after that difficult beginning. My mother was a lovely person and managed somehow to keep us together after losing my dad so recently. My sister and I haven't talked about it much over the years, so much has happened since and it all seems a long time ago now.

## Chapter Two. 'I took care of her by dragging her out of the air raid shelter.'

### Jean White's Story (Sister to Paddy).

My name is Jean White. I was evacuated with my sister Paddy in July 1940. My mother had not had long to get used to my father being dead, we'd already had to move and leave our house that we were in when he died. He had a very bad time in the First World War. He was at Gallipoli and suffered nervous trouble as a result of that and then he had also had family tragedies, his brother was killed in a road accident and his younger sister had died just before he did, so he was quite a sick man. Then he died as a result of the Munich Crisis in 1938, so we had to leave our house where we lived on the East Hill to a much smaller one, which I hated at first but then by the time I got used to it we were told we were being evacuated. I can't remember how much notice we had before we went and of course it upset my mother very much, our going, she said she never made the beds for three days. I can't remember being afraid or anything. I was fourteen at the time and I think I must have thought it was a bit of an adventure. My sister tells me that I was crying when we got there and she said, "What's the matter, don't you like it here?" but I don't remember.

We had a very nice billet to start with, with very aristocratic people. They had a nanny and a beautifully looked after house, part of which was three hundred years old with a lovely garden.

Paddy, Nanny and Jean with aristocratic family.

In the garden were lots of fruit trees and I made the mistake of eating too many plums and landed up in hospital, well it wasn't a hospital really but a nursing home attached to the hospital. When I came out there was an argument about who was going to pay the bill. Of course this family with lots of money hadn't thought twice about sending me off there, they hadn't thought about who was going to pay the bill, who paid it in the end I don't know.

We stayed in this house for about two months and it was lovely, very, very nice and then we had to move out. The excuse was that the mother was coming home from the nursing home, she actually had tuberculosis and when she came home she wanted the place quiet, so they chucked out the evacuees. We went to a young couple where the husband was a manager or foreman of an engineering works and the house was very near the works. It wasn't too bad but it was very cold because by that time it was autumn and we were also jolly hungry. We probably had school dinners but when we got home there was nobody there to give us anything to eat and my mum furnished us with a big tin of biscuits to keep us going in the evenings, it was a bit of a come down. I don't know how long we were there, probably not very long, I believe the wife was going to have a baby so they made that the excuse to get rid of us and so we were thrown out again.

The next billet was a council house and this family as far as I can make out all used the same towel and the bath water was sort of doled out. I think we had to bath in the water the washing had been done in or something. My sister got impetigo and we both had measles and I was quite ill with pneumonia and pleurisy and I had to go to hospital again but because I'd got measles they dragged me all over the country, no nursing home for me this time. First of all I went to Bishop's Stortford by ambulance but they didn't want me and in the end I landed up in an isolation hospital in Cheshunt because I was infectious. I was there for a week or two and of course I felt awful afterwards but didn't realise that meantime my mother had managed to get two rooms in Ware, it was at the time when everybody who could was advised to leave Hastings.

She suddenly arrived one day when I was back at school, as I was coming out I saw her. It was an awful shock and everybody said, "Ooh you did go white." I didn't know she was coming so it was a shock because of the suddenness of it, the suddenness of seeing her there in the street when I hadn't seen her for about seven months.

After that we lived in these two rooms in somebody else's house with my mother. I slept with her and Paddy in one room and then we had a sort of sitting room, the man who lived in the other part of the house worked at Allenbury's factory, so he was out all day and that wasn't too bad, at least we were on our own and fairly independent. My mum got the job of

Billeting Officer and used to work jolly hard, I realise that now how hard she must have worked, she used to tramp about all over the place, go everywhere on foot because she didn't have a car or anything. After a while she managed to find a furnished house and get us out of those two rooms, so we were all properly together again and that was the best of all really. The woman who owned the house went to live with her daughter down the road, so we had the whole house to ourselves.

I was always about a year older than all the other people in my form because I'd been to a private school when my father was alive and when I went to the High School the people of my age had been doing certain subjects which I hadn't touched at all. They'd all been doing Latin and geometry for a year when I got there. My sister of course was the other way round; they let her join the school when she was too young. She was the baby of the school and she always got on very well and was always ahead, she might be cleverer too. We'd only had the use of the school building part time at Ware, we had to share with Ware Grammar School for half a day and the rest of the time we were having lessons in church halls and tons of odd places but we used their playing fields. I don't think the Ware people liked us at all, everything that went wrong they blamed on to the evacuees. There wasn't much vandalism like there is now but the evacuees were blamed for anything that did happen.

I remember the air raids at Ware in 1940. We were just about to set off up the long drive to our first billet when there was this bomber, a 'dog fight' started overhead and we took shelter in the lodge, which was occupied by another couple of our girls. One of them was the Head Girl named Hannah, I was sitting on the floor and I saw her eyes get wider and wider as we heard all these planes fighting overhead.

When we stayed with the council house family before my mum came and we moved in with her, the whole family used to clear off to the shelter every night, I think they used to wait for the sirens but the sirens went every night anyway but as soon as there was any hint, at the first wail - off they went but I couldn't sleep down there and I cannot go without sleep. It wasn't an Anderson shelter it was a public shelter and people would have fights and arguments down there and it was pretty horrible and rather than put up with that I used to go home sometimes. My sister says I used to drag her with me but I can't remember that, I thought I was on my own but that was wicked I suppose because I risked the bombs rather than stay down there because it was so awful. I mean there was no way you could sleep or anything because you were sitting on the hard benches, some of the younger children had bunk beds but they weren't very comfortable either.

We thought we were being sent to a safe area but even after the time of the blitz we had doodlebugs later when they started, we had land mines too. There was a landmine in Ware Park, it hung in the trees for sometime then they went and fetched it down and found it was still likely to go off so they let it off in a gravel pit and blew everyone's windows out, I remember seeing that land mine come down during the air raid, I saw it caught in a searchlight. In our second billet we used to go into an air raid shelter with all the Firemen and it was only a tiny little shelter, which felt very crowded and airless. We were all crammed in there and one night when somebody struck a match and there was not enough oxygen to keep the match alight. Those are my memories of being bombed. I didn't feel very safe at times but I suppose I took it all very philosophically but I remember crouching on the floor and being terrified and thinking that the next minute was going to be my last.

Maybe all the bombing had stopped by the time my mother came but the doodlebugs of course were still coming over. I remember once when my sister Patricia was ill downstairs and my mother was ill upstairs and there were doodlebugs coming over and I didn't know which one to go to. My mother had quinsy and Paddy had a poisoned leg or sprained ankle, she had both while we were there, I forget which one it was but she was lying on a couch downstairs, my mother was in bed upstairs and I didn't know which one I ought to be with as the doodlebug went over but luckily it kept going. When you hear them stop then you dive for cover. There were no doodlebugs left by the end of 1944, by then they'd bombed all the places they were setting them off from but the V2's which followed were terrible; most of those went down in London. I heard the first one go off when we were at Ware, it came down in Chiswick and the yarn was that it had hit the Gas Works, they gave no warning.

I left school when I was nearly seventeen but I can't think where we were living then. I got a job in the Warite factory because I had this sort of patriotic feeling that I wanted to do some war work and I was fed up with school, so I left. When I worked at the Warite they were making plastics, it was a subsidiary of Bakelite Ltd. They made all sorts of stuff, the instrument panels and things like that for aircraft which was quite interesting and I went there fired with enthusiasm because I thought I was going to work in the factory itself but they said, "No, we don't have any women in the factory". There was one who had just got pregnant actually but I went into the works office where we used to plan the loads as they call them for the presses. They made the stuff either with paper or fabric, which was pressed with resin and you had to plan the special thickness for each load before it went into the press. Eventually they stopped me even going into the factory with messages because I used to get the most terrible colds, which seemed to be connected to me going into the factory but I was quite happy there. There was one younger person worked there otherwise most of the staff were older than me. They were a nice crowd, the person I worked with was rather funny, she used to make me laugh because her father was a gardener up at the Sanatorium and she always suspected everybody of having TB, whenever anybody coughed she went 'ugh' gave all these frowns and went 'huh'.

When my mother was coming home and Paddy was coming back with the school I wanted to come home. I had to go and see some official to get away because I was in a war job, we were doing war work and my boss didn't want to let me go. He said I would get called up and have to go in the ATS or something. So I went to see this official, something to do with Labour and told him I was an evacuee and wanted to go home now. That was in October 1944, so he let me go. When I got home to Hastings nobody cared what I was doing, nobody said I'd have to go into the ATS or anything else, nobody took any interest and eventually I got at job at the Post Office as a telephonist.

We went back to our original house, it had some damage but had survived the bombing, and it was OK. Coming home was lovely, lovely; the first sight of the sea was marvellous, we always missed the sea. I did come home once while we were away and stayed with my grandfather who had been bombed out, he was living in our house with his housekeeper and I came and stayed with him. I remember being so excited when I first saw the sea then. There wasn't any bombing on that occasion but my grandfather was a bit strict, he was very Victorian, and you know, "Take your feet off the rungs of the chairs". I was playing Patience on the day I was due to come back and he was annoyed because I was playing Patience when I was just going to go. Whether he had a premonition I don't know because he died and I never saw him again; whether he thought he might not be here when I came back who knows but people do have these feelings don't they? I can't remember the eventual journey back as the others had already come and I had to cross London on my own and the war was still on. Paddy went back to the High School and had a jolly good time as far as I can make out.

I don't know what gave me the idea of becoming a telephonist; someone must have suggested it I suppose. I stayed there until the beginning of 1947 when I had 'flu very badly and couldn't stand it any longer, I'd get to screaming point, it was nerve racking if you weren't feeling quite the ticket, some girls would start screaming or crying. We used to do a long stint without a break, you'd finish up with all the plugs on your board used up, and it was like a lot of knitting in front of you. After the 'flu I got depressed, I just couldn't stand it and I left. I had a few weeks off and then went into the Food Office, rationing was still on but it was calmer and I was quite happy there.

I wouldn't want to leave Hasting again only for holidays. I think I'd feel worse if I had to leave it now than I did then, children are more adaptable. As long as I got enough to eat and someone to look after me I was all right but I did miss my mum, I did, I did, and it wasn't long after I'd lost my dad just before the war. It was such a shock when I suddenly saw my mum coming up the road at Ware.

My experiences gave me a lot insight into how other people live but I don't long for better things, I've always been fairly contented and I don't envy other people much. There was a nanny looking after us in the first place where the mother was ill and the father was away and I found out afterwards he had to go to the War Office every day. I can't say that I was particularly fond of them, the only one I really liked was the smallest child, he was only five but I've forgotten his name. I've since followed the family and they all died quite young but I've kept a photo taken in 1940, I've not kept in touch with them at all but G- the one I liked, he was a sweetie, a dear little soul. But the others were getting a bit of a snobby attitude I think. I remember going to a party, there were all these kids with their nannies and they were very rude to us while we were there. It was because we were evacuees; the two we were living with didn't want to be associated with us while we were there obviously. One of the nannies tried to excuse them by saying, "You often find the upper class children are like this, they are a bit more rude than the average child." There wasn't anybody at any of the billets that I felt particularly at ease with. The council house family were quite nice but what my mother would call rough and ready; they weren't very particular which is probably why we became so ill there. I suppose they did their best but they were probably hard up and they weren't our sort of people.

I don't know that being evacuated affected me particularly any more than ordinary life would affect you. I mean you learn by experience, don't you wherever you are? I don't think it affected me in any sort of dramatic way. By 1948 I was married for the first time, my husband left me and I married again but have no children. I can't really say whether evacuation was a positive or negative effect. When I think about it all now it affects me much more than it did then because I had to leave home but only someone else could say if it may have affected me more than the rough and tumble of life but I do hate people leaving, I hate people going away. I always feel a bit apprehensive when other people go away; I feel I may never see them again. Maybe that has to do with people going away in the war and I never saw them again. I can't remember thinking I would never see my mother again when I went away but of course I would think that now, maybe I wasn't as pessimistic when I was a child, I think when you're younger you just accept things.

I can't remember feeling particularly responsible for my sister, I led her a terrible life really, teasing her and trying to frighten her about things. I'm terribly ashamed of it now, I wonder she speaks to me but I suppose the psychology of it was rivalry, a kind of jealousy. I was the only grandchild on both sides for five years before she came along, then we had to share things; that was at the back of it. We're great friends now, we don't see very much of each other but we talk on the phone each week but I don't know why she speaks to me, I really did lead her an awful life. I took care of her by dragging her out of the air raid shelter, I don't think I was very responsible but I daresay if anyone else had attacked Paddy, I would have stuck up for her.

## Chapter 3. 'It wasn't what I'd been accustomed to.'
## Jean Scrivener's Story.

My name is Jean Scrivener, I live in Hastings and I wouldn't have been in this part of the world if it hadn't been for the First World War. My father realised he had a service to give because he had experience with motor transport; he was well into his thirties when he volunteered with three young children and spent most of his war in the Middle East in Mesopotamia. When he came home having been very badly injured by the Turks his health was threatened and it was suggested he might survive a little longer if he came to the South Coast of England, which he did. Three years later I was born, which meant that I was the child of older parents with brothers and a sister of twenty, fourteen and sixteen.

When war broke out in September 1939, my mother was a billeting officer with the Women's Royal Voluntary Service in Hastings and I remember the actual day war was declared. We had just received a group of evacuees from Deptford in London, but a lot of them were originally from Ireland. My mother had carefully toured our area consisting of big Victorian houses and although ours was a family house they had mostly been converted into flats. We were expecting children, but to her horror, mothers with young babies turned up, who were much, much harder to place and caused a great many difficulties. My mother took in two mothers, each with a young baby. There was a lot of improvisation, a laundry basket being rigged up for one baby and a drawer for another to sleep in, that sort of thing. They stayed with us until almost Christmas.

It certainly turned our family life upside down, because I think now they would be viewed as rather feckless. My mother, who was a very experienced sort of person, tried to help them to get a little bit of order into their lives. There has to be a certain amount of planning if you've got three women trying to share your kitchen and you're a mother trying to cope for your own family, but they were easy going, very, very easy going. I think we made them happy and I think they coped but they gradually drifted back and by Christmas they'd all gone and our family life carried on fairly normally. That was my first experience of evacuation.

Of course, by the next spring there was talk of the danger of invasion and on the 21st July 1940 we ourselves were evacuated. I was still at primary school and I suppose up until then I'd had a very simple but very happy, very secure family life. My brother and my sister were still living at home and I had an older brother who had married in 1936. I was lucky because I did have holidays with my parents, very few children had in those days. I'd been to Scotland, which was quite an event, and I had stayed on my own with members of the family without my parents, and been away for about a week before they picked me up. So I was lucky in that I had had a fair amount of independence and I feel it helped to prepare me for being evacuated.

I went with my primary school in my last year there and I'd already taken the so-called eleven plus examination but we hadn't yet heard the results. As we pulled out in a Special train from Hastings station, there was actually a 'dog fight' in the sky overhead and we looked up, not realising this was the beginning of the Battle of Britain. By devious means the train was routed right through to Bedfordshire without us having to change.

The first place we arrived at was Ampthill in Bedfordshire, which was a sort of dispersal centre. We were unloaded there and we went into some sort of Town Hall. Then the different groups broke up because we were going to villages and it was impossible for the whole of our school to go to one village, they were just too small to accommodate us. So the older children in the top two or three forms went with a few of the teachers to a village called Clockhill and the younger children went to a little village called Houghton Conquest a few miles away but incredibly difficult to access because there was no sort of direct transport. When we were being gathered up there, the one thing that I thought was a terrible indignity was that they checked our hair for lice and nits and I felt most indignant. I came from a good home and I can't imagine that there could have been one child in the school who would have had a problem with a head infection; I came from quite a nice area and it wasn't a thing that I was aware of and I remember being a little hurt.

People came and took ones and twos away, and I was collected by a young woman with a baby in her arms and went to a little cottage on The Green. It was really quite a culture shock because I'd grown up in a big Victorian house with a bathroom and hot running water and had a bedroom of my own with pleasant comforts like a fridge, which was very unusual so I realised that we had a reasonable life style. Then here I was in a little cottage and it was a bit of a shock because there was no electricity; they cooked by paraffin and to this day I just hate the smell of paraffin, that smell as the stove is extinguished. There was a little house up the garden which was rather a terrifying thing and I realised I'd got to wash at the kitchen sink and I wasn't used to not having privacy.

When I wrote my letter home and said that I'd arrived I did not say that there were problems; I just said that I'd arrived safely. We did have our own class teacher with us and I think she soon realised this wasn't the ideal place; it wasn't what I'd been accustomed to and within about three days, I found myself billeted with the Headmaster of the village school and his wife and I felt at home there, it was quite comfortable but I don't know how it came about because I have no recollection that I complained. Apparently their live-in maid from the village was asked to go home and sleep so that I could have her room. By the time I got there in July the school holidays had already started but it wasn't a problem because we found ways of filling the time and all through the end of July and August our teachers took us on walks in the lovely woods; in those days you could just wander. I went fishing and things like that as I had done at home, we sort of wandered about and had a holiday there. A friend of mine from the same school was billeted at the far end of the village and we'd sort of meet up with each other, and then when the village school re-opened we started classes with them. There were also some London evacuees there, which was why accommodation was at such a premium. Then the exam results came through and my mother wrote saying I had been awarded a special place at the Hastings High School as a result of the scholarship.

By early October arrangements were made for me to transfer to Ware Grammar School, and by then of course term had already begun. I can't remember how we got there except that it was a cross-country journey; three of us went from the village. I found myself being taken this time to a modern semi-detached house in Trinity Road where there was a young couple, very much like the London evacuees that came to us at Hastings originally, easy going and Irish again, strangely enough, with a young baby. They hadn't got around to making any blackout, so you had to go upstairs and wash in the dark and get into bed in the dark. It wasn't a very pleasant experience but the friend, the one I'd gone with from school, was billeted four doors lower down and I used to call for her on the way to school. She was living with a delightful older gentleman; a retired artist and his housekeeper who was a very nice middle-aged lady and Kathleen my friend was terribly happy there. They cottoned on where I was, and realised straightaway that it was not a suitable place to be, and immediately it seemed to be arranged quite amicably for me to join Kathleen. We had to share a double bed fitted into a little box-room, which you literally crawled over to get into bed, but we were really happy there and it was more like what I was used to. Kathy and I got on very well and that first Christmas my parents came down, made the journey to visit us but I'd been lucky, because we were very good at corresponding. My father was the one who kept in touch he was the good correspondent. My brother who was in the Navy also wrote, we couldn't phone because we just didn't have them. I had a Postal Order every fortnight for half-a-crown, which was adequate to buy my stamps and my toothpaste and my little treats. I had to learn to manage money and not spend it all in one go, and I even saved a little and thought about things I could do. With the rationing we got very excited if we could find some things that were short. My parents came to visit me that Christmas for the day with gifts and things but they were caught up in the Blitz on London going back and had a pretty awful experience. They were just trapped down in the Underground and I know that the hat my mother was wearing had little cinders all over the brim.

In those early nights at Ware we sat up under the stairs because you could see the fires in London and you could hear the blitz. Every now and then a stray bomb or two dropped in Ware, which was really an accident, it wasn't intentional but then we did sit up, there was one in Muswell Hill. My mother made me a wonderful garment called a 'siren suit', Mr. Churchill sponsored them; it was made in blue and my sister embroidered my initial on the pocket very beautifully. It had a huge zip right up and a hood lined with red, I could put it on over my nightclothes when I got up to shelter. There wasn't a public shelter near to us so we went downstairs and sat under the stairs because it was considered the safest place where you were most likely to survive. So we had a lot of broken nights and that siren suit comes back to me, which my parents thought might be a useful thing and yes it was, but it was also a great comfort to me. There was always this sense of danger around but I don't think we were terribly worried for ourselves but much more concerned about the people back home because of the 'hit and run' raids and one or two of our girls did lose parents. We were very concerned when the news came through that there had been a raid and I was also very concerned for my brother at sea on the Convoys and we waited very anxiously to hear from him. He wrote the most marvellous letters to me; I've still got one or two of them. I always sent him a copy of my school reports and he was always encouraging me to do more, never allowing me to be complacent but congratulating me also on what I had done.

By the next spring things were rather different at home and it was decided that it was safe enough for me to go home for a holiday. I can't honestly say I was homesick as such because I had had the experience of being away and one knew that one needed to be there. If you'd stayed at home it would be dangerous and there'd be no education. You just felt it was right and you were doing the right thing and what was expected of you but I did start going home for Christmas. My mother came down to actually fetch me, and a couple of other girls, to escort us back by train. We went up to Liverpool Street station and crossed to Victoria by Underground. Within about a year I think we realised this was a lot of expense so we started to go home alone by train. The last time my mother escorted us she said, "Right, I'll be there but you take me." So I had to take the initiative and I remember I went down the Underground at Liverpool Street and had to make sure I got to the Inner Circle and I can remember the relief when we found the right station. The main instruction was that if a raid was on, it would be displayed in the Underground, so you stayed down, you didn't come up. I'd be about thirteen by then and quite a little group of us were trusted to do it together, we knew the ropes, we went across to Victoria and down to Hastings.

When I went home I became used to seeing the upper windows of the house broken, just nailed up with board and one with a compulsory piece of glass in, in case there was a fire... one window with that nasty semi-opaque glass in. Then when things got very bad the ceilings were down. It was one of those big Victorian houses with a basement which you could have reinforced, so one holiday when I went home that had been done and two huge tree trunks had been put from the bay window to the back with five uprights supporting them. The thing was, you then had to display a notice outside saying 'You May Shelter Here'. You knew exactly what to do if you were out during an air raid; you just went into the nearest place that you could shelter because you were aware of the risk. My parents had had to take their bed down there and were really just camping out in the basement because the rest of the house was more or less derelict. I think there was only one other house inhabited in the whole of our road and the number went up to fifty. We shared a stirrup pump with the Catholic Church down the road and when my mother took it up to our porch the priest took it back to the church. My mother argued that domestic homes were much more important but the priest didn't agree with her.

My father was in the Home Guard; mother was still doing a lot of work in the WRVS helping with the British Restaurants, which they set up at Tower Road School. When I was at home during the holidays and she was on duty, I would go there with her and help her out. She was also helping at a little place in Kings Road, where the soldiers could drop in. They could have a cup of tea, listen to a radio and have their socks mended, so I would go there with her when I was on holiday. Sometimes we'd go to the Home Guard area where my father was on duty and make cocoa, I got good at mixing cocoa; it was an awful job to get it to go at first with a little drop of milk. I became very aware of what was going on at home but I wouldn't have missed going back to Hastings, I just had to put up with it. I began to understand by that time that basically it wasn't so much for safety as for education that we remained at Ware. I've said many times to friends since the good thing that came out of the experience was that it made me appreciate my home, because you learned to conform and to live in other people's homes in a way they expected. I learned that very quickly.

That was a very happy billet with the artist, then sadly he developed cancer. We knew something was wrong. It wasn't talked about in those days but we realised because he needed nursing and, sadly, his housekeeper had to say she couldn't cope, so I was re-billeted when I returned from holiday with a girl I hadn't known called Pearl, at a different place with a couple named Snow, quite old and very kindly. We shared a great big feather bed and were taught how to shake it up every morning. Again conditions weren't too good, we had to wash in the kitchen but they gave us privacy. On Friday nights they brought out the bath and put it in front of the fire and we took it in turns to have the first go and it was topped up for the next. But certainly it was a very secure place and we enjoyed life with them.

After about a year unfortunately Mrs Snow was ill and at one point she went into hospital but rather than us have to leave she arranged for us to stay with her married daughter about four miles away in Hoddesden, a delightful lady who had also married a man called Mr Snow and had a little girl of three. We spent a week with them; we knew her well from her visits home and we used to take a bus back into Ware to get to school. We returned to the first Mrs Snow when she came out but it was obvious that her health was deteriorating and so we had yet another billet. We were moved this time to a Council house, the amenities were there but it wasn't a happy place. Mr Wallace was a charming little man, but he was quite hen pecked by his wife Hilda, he was in the Auxiliary Fire Service and they had adopted a little girl called Margaret. With hindsight I realise that Margaret had problems and what she wanted was attention and she made life pretty grim for us. She was five and we were fourteen or fifteen and she would come up very stealthily and pinch us because she resented us and that made life pretty difficult, we just learned to cope with it but it wasn't easy. Our foster parents stuck up for her; it would be our fault but Pearl and I were incredibly loyal to each other. Our foster mother Hilda Wallace was a funny lady but he was rather sweet, very henpecked, poor old Mr Wallace but we rather liked him, they had to just accept us as the status quo. I mean I just knew I'd got to stick it out and cope with it, I didn't whinge I thought, "Well, this is it!" Had we known, we would probably have made much more fuss of Margaret their adopted daughter if we had understood the psychology but she was so spiteful; it was difficult. The Wallaces themselves were not unkind but unpredictable and indifferent. I can remember her mum used to come and she didn't approve of us; she thought we were a burden to her daughter, you had this feeling of being unwanted but you saw there was no alternative, there was nowhere else to go. It united us, we knew we couldn't afford to fall out, we stuck together Pearl and I; we really did. We did what we could for each other and shared everything like the bit of housework we had to do. One thing we couldn't wait to be allowed to do was to make the porridge, which was cooked in a saucepan with a 'pot-mender' in it. Younger people don't know about them, but in those days when things were expensive, you had a thing called a 'pot-mender', it was two washers held together by a bit of metal, which meant the porridge stuck to the saucepan and there's nothing as foul as burnt porridge and if we could get there and offer to stir it we didn't get burnt porridge. We learned little wrinkles like that.

We did get facilities for doing our homework, and Mrs Wallace was an 'out-worker' for a glove factory in Hertford and she used to make gloves for five and sixpence a dozen, which was five-pence halfpenny a pair. They were very tedious and in the construction of a well-made glove, it has a strip down and a diamond called a quirk. The tedious bit was sewing all those little quirks into the strip. It was all done by hand at five pence halfpenny a pair to make a little extra. I was quite handy with a needle so she would allow me to sew in those quirks, which was quite devious really because she'd pay me a halfpenny a pair but it was rather thrilling for me at the time because I was actually earning some money, but it was sweated labour, wasn't it!

One nice thing about it was that they had chickens and Mrs Wallace, the hen-pecking wife, placed sets of duck eggs under a hen and we were fascinated by it all. It was most interesting when they hatched out. I can remember this quite clearly on 6th June 1944; that was D-Day. There was the excitement of seeing these tiny ducklings hatch and then we set off for school and there were planes flying overhead, droves of them and underneath the wings they were painted with blue and white stripes which we'd never seen before, we'd been used to camouflaged planes. Of course then the announcement came out that day that the invasion had taken place, so it stuck very clearly in my mind and I began to think, "Right, the invasion has come, perhaps soon something will begin to happen, perhaps we can see our way towards the end."

Our education at Ware wasn't easy either, and we learned later that the host school resented us. Ware Grammar School had already had a big invasion from London, so the London evacuees were sharing the school as well but by 1944 a lot of them had disappeared and the few that remained had become integrated with them. We had the use of the school building in the afternoons and in the morning we made do around the town. I remember having lessons in the Congregational Church Hall and the Church itself.

There could be as many as three classes going on, you could have French up in the choir stalls, English in the gallery and another subject in the main body of the church. We had some of the first wireless lessons in the church as well, "How Things Began" on a rather cracked old portable radio belonging to one of the staff. In the church hall they set up a meals system and we could have our midday meal there which cost four-pence a day. I suppose really considering the wartime they weren't bad. It helped our foster parents that we ate out midday.

To reach the church hall you went up a little narrow passage from the road and at the bottom of that passage there was a baker's shop and the smell of buns freshly baked was absolutely wonderful but we were not supposed to leave the area of the church and the church hall and the tiny asphalt area in front of it. It was a terrific dare to sneak down to the bakers and try to buy something and just hope you didn't meet a member of the staff, because it really was forbidden. Then in the afternoon we made our way to the school itself, where we had access to laboratories and things that we couldn't do in the church hall. We carried a great weight of books because we had no desks. Everything had to be kept in our billets and you had to be very careful in the morning to take with you all that you needed for the whole day's lessons. We carried very heavy satchels and I had a drooping shoulder with the weight of mine and was told you must alternate your satchel; it made me very responsible because I'd got to have everything I needed with me. We had quite a good rapport with the staff because after all they were 'in loco parentis'. I think I had a much better rapport than I

32

would have done if I'd just been at an ordinary school; it just happened it never occurred to me to do otherwise. By now certain girls were leaving. They were going off to join their parents in other parts of England, for instance, and a few were drifting back to Hastings. There was some attempt to set up education for them, but it just didn't occur to me to ask to go back, I knew that that was where my parents needed me to be for their own sort of peace of mind and to get my education, so I stayed on. With the drift back a few of our teachers returned, which put stress on the others because they had to teach subjects that were not their norm. I can remember Miss Bartholomew, who was our science teacher, a charming little lady, coming to me because by then I was one of the older girls and saying, "Jean, I've got to do square roots with the second year, can you remind me?" There was this great sort of trusting nice atmosphere between us.

We had a guide company and I joined because I was at the age and there were no leaders available so it was the older girls from the 6th form who ran it and it was a rattling good guide company. We used to hold it in the gym and it was a very important part of our life because you had very little social life in the war. It was a super company and it was very well run, the only thing was, we'd got nobody who could test us for badges, and the Commissioner had to come in from Much Haddam, because there was nobody local, so we ran a good company. Then we would join up with the Ware guides for certain things and I've still got a programme for a concert we gave during the war between us.

When the numbers really were dropping very considerably; most of the teachers returned to Hastings, leaving just a couple to keep an eye on those that were left and we were incorporated into the Ware Grammar School. It was lovely because we had the use of the school all day instead of this making do in church halls. I think, if anything, we probably got a better education then because of the better facilities, relieved of the misery of camping out. Pearl had left by then; she'd gone off to an aunt in Littlehampton rather than back to Hastings. It was an interesting experience actually being a member of Ware Grammar School, we continued wearing our uniforms and I think there was a member of our liaison staff that helped teach them as well as us.

By the summer term of 1945 the doodlebugs were starting to come over. I'd actually been playing cricket for my house up on the lovely playing fields at Ware, which were quite a way from the school and when I got home there was a telegram for me from my father saying 'recommend return home'. I didn't really know why but obviously that was what he wanted me to do and I can remember making an appointment to go and see the Headmistress of Ware Grammar School and saying, "I've had this telegram from my father, who thinks it's right that I should return home". So that was it and I literally went back to my billet and packed my case. It turned out that he had been watching the track of the doodlebugs and he realised that Ware was becoming a dangerous place to be, you were more at risk than in Hastings as they were passing over unless they were shot down or were faulty. Of course there were the mysterious V2 rockets we didn't know about at the time which were kept very much hush, hush, we weren't told about them but they were also starting to come over. This was my particular call and I can remember winding things up on my bed and saying goodbye and thank you. In those days you packed your own case and belongings and took yourself off on the train. That would have been in July 1945 when the school holiday was looming and after that I started at the Hastings High School building that following autumn. It was the first time I'd ever set foot in it though I'd been a pupil of the Hastings High School all those years. I can remember the thrill of, "I'm home to stay" rather than being just a holiday, it isn't just for a period. I remember saying to my mother, "May I have another piece of bread?" She was quite horrified and said "But this is your home, all the while we've got bread, you can have it." It was three slices in my billet, one with a scrape of margarine and two with a scrape of jam or visa versa, never the two and to this day I adore bread and butter and jam because for years you only had one or the other. I think it was a case of making do. I've got to be honest and say that we weren't really hungry but there were times when we would have loved a little more. It was due to rationing and after all foster parents aren't going to make quite the same efforts. I think we might have been more spoilt if we'd been with our own parents, who would probably have gone without, not that one would have wanted them to but they would. I think quite often we would have liked a little more but you accepted it and that was it, although my mother was quite horrified that I needed to ask if I could have another piece of bread. It was what made her understand that we had been very restricted in the last billet. I went to college when I got home which meant by the time I left college I'd spent more than half my life away from home. You felt you'd missed a lot. Yes, I did feel that because my father was older you see, by the time I left school and went to college he was sixty-two years old. I never married, probably because of course being the youngest I was the one who stayed at home and cared for my parents and later on my two older brothers as well. Yes, it has rather dominated my life, I don't mind admitting that it has. It never occurred to me to do otherwise. You see, they had made a lot of sacrifices for me. In those days you had to pay for your tuition at college and my father literally kept on working through the war to replace a younger man, which probably wouldn't have happened otherwise. That's the only reason that my parents were allowed to remain in Hastings because he was contributing to the war effort. He was an engineer, and when he came up to retirement age he stayed on and ran the pumping station in the park, keeping the water supply going. That's the only reason they stayed in Hastings, otherwise they would have left the town too. Anybody who wasn't necessary and vital to running the amenities and the war effort had been evacuated. My mother had always been a housewife but very involved with the community, she was always very involved.

Evacuation certainly added to my experience. I told you how when I was living with Mrs Snow and she became ill we spent a week with her daughter and we got to know her very well. Last year I was able to go and visit her, I've kept in touch with her every year. She is now ninety-one years old and lives with her daughter, so last year I went down to the New Forest to visit her, looked her up. It was lovely to meet up with her. I shan't go again, I don't need to but it was something I felt I had to do... having written all those years and she said, "You'd be so welcome to come." They did actually come down here at one point when her husband was convalescent. Pearl, the girl that I shared a bed with is living in Chichester and I called to see her as well last year. I did make some very deep friendships, which have survived. Her case was very different because she had a very sad family background, her mother died and quite a substantial allowance went with her and the aunts who cared for her wanted that more than her. She was telling me last year that her evacuation was the happiest time of her life because she escaped, she found it the most stable and happy time of her life. I was a year older, which was a lot when you were at school and if anything I think I protected her a little. I was not homesick as such but I knew I would much rather be at home but we all knew that Ware was where we were expected to be and needed to be and we just put up with it, we didn't complain. Now I find myself thinking that modern children wouldn't cope with it in the same way because of the type of life they lead, I don't think they could. They're much more concerned with getting their own way and would have far less thought, I think, for what was the right thing to do and what was the necessary thing to do compared to what they wanted, that would be predominant in their thoughts in this modern permissive society, but I think they have a very tough time, I mean the teenagers. It can be very difficult bringing your children up in today's society. You see we had our parameters; we knew what they were. I feel that was a great advantage, easier for me and for many others. I had such a secure and supportive home and family and very good correspondence backwards and forwards all the time, but they didn't tell us the worst things. Oh no, they kept those to themselves.

My mother was Church of England and very involved with the church and the Mother's Union, in fact she was the Enrolling Member. It was Trinity church and that area served a lot of rather small, poor houses and she did a lot of good social work among some of the young women there. I remember her saying when she knew we would be going away to be in somebody else's home, "Now, wherever you go, if they worship, you go with them". So I was a Methodist and I pumped the organ at the Congregational church but the last ones were not religious, so then Pearl and I used to take ourselves along to church. On the whole it was quite a positive experience because you had to come to be so independent I learned quite a few things like how to be happy to do anything to 'muck in' and wash up. The very first billet, where I was for a few days, I can remember the lady asking me to dust, she gave me a duster and I didn't know what to do with it and I just wiped the seat of a chair. I really couldn't see what else I had to do because our home just ran very efficiently, we had domestic help and that was it; I think she realised that I wasn't quite sure what to do. When I went back to Clophill I found it very difficult even to orientate myself because the old school had been pulled down, which would have been my landmark so it took me a long while to even organise myself; it had changed so much. It was ages before I could find anything familiar. I went back to Ware recently as well. Of course the Ware Grammar School has completely disappeared, I found it completely gone, it's just a modern block now. It was very, very, evocative to go back. It was something I felt I had to do. I don't need to go again and I'm sure I shan't, now that I've got it out of my system, but it was one of those things that I just had to do.

I had a lot more respect afterwards for Miss Fanny Commin, the Headmistress. I didn't at the time; I found her very enigmatic and hated the way she sat there grinning when you had medicals and she had to sit in and that sort of thing. But when she died, we got a sub committee together. As the Old Girls we thought we ought to do something about it, and we turned out some of her letters which I was asked to read and so on. It came to light that she had a very tough time when she took us to Ware. They didn't want us, they'd already had the London evacuees, they didn't want us and she had to really fight apparently for us to get what few amenities we had. Now we never knew that, and with hindsight I could see that she was quite a wise sort of woman. The teachers were 'in loco parentis' but didn't get involved in our emotions, nobody thought about things like that... you didn't have troubles, so, I just got on with my life. Nobody knew about it, about being traumatized, it never occurred, it wasn't understood; you just had to get on with your life. You didn't expect any sympathy for feelings, we were all in the same boat, everybody had got their own problems to get on with that's how I saw it, although I think if we'd really had problems maybe we could have gone to someone.

# Chapter 4. 'What I found so hard was the cold almost indifference to us.'

## Keith's story.

My name is Keith. I'm a retired country parson and I live in Taunton, Somerset with my wife Sheila. I was born and brought up in Hastings Sussex, and my family consisted of my father, my mother and my sister Sylvia and myself.

Keith with his sister Sylvia on the West Hill at Hastings.

We were a poor family, my father was a bus conductor and my mother went out cleaning to keep the home together.

I went to the local infants' and primary school and then, having passed the eleven plus selection, started at the Hastings Grammar School in September 1938. Grammar School before the war was very much a structured, formal organisation and in many ways, for a new little boy starting, very intimidating. Masters wore gowns and there was a much more rigid atmosphere and rigid discipline than existed in the primary school, which continued for many years in the Public Schools. but I think it has now gone throughout the country and things are much more relaxed. When I started at the Grammar School I have one particular memory. Coming from such a poor home my parents couldn't afford the regulation school blazer and I was the only boy in the class not to have the very smart blazer for some months. A feeling of being left out resulted from that and I felt rather different from the other boys, but that was soon forgotten when I was eventually kitted out in my full uniform. I do remember one particular occasion when some boys took my very nice new school cap and threw it away, and my parents had to replace it, and a school cap cost money and that produced some distress.

I wasn't particularly happy in the childhood home because, sadly, my father drank too much, which often resulted in him coming home and having a row with my mother and there would be unpleasant scenes, which for a small growing child caused much distress. In fact it was the particular bugbear of my growing life and has haunted me ever since, so that at my ripe old age of seventy-three I cannot even now enjoy going into a pub for a drink. Our parents weren't very happy but we did have a sense of security and a feeling of belonging that the war was soon to take away from us. Life at the new school was very absorbing and a completely new experience to those of us who had just started. We learned subjects we'd never heard of before like Latin and languages, and it was a time of challenge; but at the same time it opened our eyes to a new world, then came the war. My father, during the First World War, was a cook on a destroyer in the Royal Navy. He was present at the Battle of Jutland and also I believe witnessed (from 'off shore' on the destroyer) the disastrous landing at Gallipoli. He told me during my boyhood about these things and showed me the medals that he had got during the war. My mother's brothers were in the war, one of them in the army in the trenches.

When the Second World War broke out my grandparents who lived in Highbury, in London, because of the imminent threat of warfare and whatever that was going to imply, came down to stay in our very small house in Hastings. It was a very tiny house, two up and two down. They were looking for somewhere to live nearby but we were all there together in that tiny house the actual week war that broke out. Until then I don't think I'd ever left home for any reason, but on this occasion the very week war broke out I was at camp with the local Boys' Brigade at Crowhurst near Hastings. One of the things we did at the Boys' Brigade in those days was to learn semaphore signaling with flags. Some of the lads had gone into the village shop from the fields where we were camping and signaled to us with three letters WAR.

We at once upped camp and returned home. It was then that I discovered that our grandparents had come and were staying with us in our tiny little house. How on earth we managed for those weeks I have no idea. I was a choirboy in the local church and on that Sunday morning when war was announced I was singing in the service as usual when the churchwarden came and whispered to the vicar. The vicar then said, "It has just been announced that war has been declared, I think it would be wise if all the choir boys went home immediately." I went home to find my mother and my grandmother in tears, and my father and my grandfather trying to put up black curtains at the windows because of the possibility of being identified for air raids. From that moment on, throughout the war, every night you had to black out the windows so that no light shone out. I'd hardly got home when we heard for the first time the air raid siren, this was literally minutes after the declaration of war. I remember distinctly seeing a policeman riding by on a bicycle blowing a whistle, shouting to everybody in a frantic voice, "Take cover, take cover". In fact that was a false alarm, there was an unidentified aircraft over Eastbourne but that was the first time we were to hear the ominous sound of the air raid warning.

After war was declared life went on for some time much the same. We went off to school and in our childhood minds we knew very little of the politics of the early war, in fact it was known I believe as the 'Phoney War.' It wasn't until the beginning early months of 1940 that we became very much and very closely aware of what the war was beginning to mean. In May 1940 there was the evacuation from Dunkirk, and I have a particular memory of standing on the beach by the Fish-market at Hastings with my mother, watching the small boats bringing the soldiers back from the beaches at Dunkirk. It was a very moving experience. Incidentally it was while standing there and watching these poor soldiers come back that I cut my leg rather badly on some barbed wire and had to go and have some plaster put on it at the local chemist. But the memory of those soldiers stepping out of the boats has remained with me ever since. That was in May 1940.

There is another memory of June 1940 that I shall never forget. The whole school was summoned into the school hall one morning and the Head Master accompanied by some of the senior Masters spoke to the whole school. He said that we were in great danger because it was likely that at any moment the Germans would invade our country and being on the coast they would soon arrive into our town. If the invasion took place any day in the coming week, we were if it was humanly possible, to come to school as usual and to do everything not to worry our parents who were feeling the great strain of what was happening in the war.

He also announced that in a month's time plans had been made for the whole school to be evacuated away from the danger area of Hastings to St Albans in Hertfordshire, where every effort would be made to continue our schooling and homes would be found for us. We were given letters announcing all this to take home to our parents. Parents had to make the very difficult decision whether to keep their children with them in the town, not knowing what the immediate future would bring, or to part with them, and let them be evacuated. Ours decided that my sister and I should go, my sister with the High School for girls went to Ware, in Hertfordshire, and I was evacuated with my school to St Albans, some sixteen miles away.

The day of evacuation was Sunday 21$^{st}$ July 1940, and we stood at Hastings station with our parents and had sad goodbyes but I know that we as children were feeling rather more excited than distressed at the big adventure that was going to happen to us. I remember one particular aspect of it was that all my parents could afford was a very small case from Marks & Spencers in which all my worldly possessions were packed. I took this little cardboard case together with a carrier bag given to us by the authorities containing such strange things as tins of condensed milk and packets of biscuits.

We got on the train and, being boys of twelve and thirteen years old, had fun most of the way, some of us were playing cards and some were running up and down the corridors. The train went straight through London but it wasn't until we arrived at St Albans that Sunday afternoon when we were deposited in St Peter's church hall and realised that we weren't going back that I felt more bereft than I have ever done at almost any other moment in my life. It was the first time I had been separated from my mother and I felt it dreadfully.

We stood around, and local worthies, Billeting Officers as they were called, arranged that we should go to one house or another. I was sent with a friend called Eric to a house some five miles out of St Albans in a very well to do and prosperous district. The people ran an electrical business in the town and were obviously moneyed. They had three sons, the eldest son was serving in the war, and another lad who was in his teens was at the local Public School, and there was George aged eight, who right from the first proved himself to be very much a spoiled brat and made life very painful and very difficult for my friend Eric and myself. The house as I say was very prosperous, I lost count of the rooms but they had an enormous garden and kept two hundred chickens and we were expected each morning to go out and collect the eggs and clean out the chickens before breakfast. I didn't mind this so much but what I found so hard as I lived in this home was the cold almost indifference to us that the family had. They seemed totally unable to express any kind of emotion at all.

We were extremely well fed and we had a beautiful bedroom, but the hard thing to endure, particularly coming from a poor, intimate loving home was the cold indifference of this one. There was a daughter called Peggy who was secretary to the business. She was the only one who seemed to have any warmth about her at all, and she would often sit and talk to us; otherwise we were treated almost as though we did not exist. Our food was put in front of us, our bedrooms were cleaned, our beds changed and our washing done almost as though we weren't there. We ate with the family but as I say their relations one to another were not very forthcoming and the youngest child George, who was the apple of his mother's eye was a beastly little child, and made life very difficult for Eric and myself.

In August and September 1940 the blitz began on London and you could see the flames when we looked out at night. Now, as I say, this was a very prosperous house and they had one room which was the billiard room with a full size billiard table and we were in fact allowed to play billiards in there, which we spent many hours doing. Eric and I were in there quietly on our own when a German plane was brought down in the field next door to the house. Suddenly there was this enormous noise and we thought the end of the world had come. We dived under the billiard table and the plane crashed in the field outside. We were not allowed to go and see it. Another memory was one day we were waiting at the local bus stop to get a bus back into St Albans and a Royal Air Force trailer came along with a Hienkel aircraft, a German Heinkel that had been brought down on it. My friend and I immediately jumped on the trailer because it had stopped for a moment, tore off a lot of fabric as a souvenir and jumped back off again. We cherished that bit of German aircraft we had for quite a long time.

The family took us to school each morning when they went into St Albans. Our school had taken over the local non-conformist chapel, very near to The St Albans School and all close to the Abbey. Lessons were very difficult because some days we couldn't find any room to have a lesson in, mornings we were in the non-conformist chapel and in the afternoons we were in the Public School during their sports activities.

The main experience, of course, of this time was the persistence of feeling totally lonely and cut off and isolated. I still possess some loving letters I had from my mother assuring us that we were very much in their thoughts. My father meantime had joined the local Fire Service and was very much involved in wartime call-outs and it was in fact a distressing time for everyone. Only twice in that household where we lived did I see any real emotion, and, goodness knows it was for a good enough reason! The son who was in the war came back from France from St Valerie actually near Dunkirk and he came in looking absolutely dreadful and totally exhausted, burst into tears and put his arms around his mother. The other time when there was emotion in that very cold household... we came down to breakfast one morning to find the family in tears, the father had died in his sleep during the night. I remember particularly the daughter Peggy being dreadfully upset. Consequently it was decided that now the father had died they couldn't really manage to keep evacuees any more and we would have to move. So in January 1941, we moved, we went to separate accommodation. I moved to a house above a shop right near the centre of St Albans, very close to the Abbey.

This was a totally different household. There were four of us evacuees and their own teen-aged son, and the woman who looked after us our foster mother was a very happy-go-lucky, untidy but loving person. Although we lived in extraordinarily unkempt and untidy conditions she did offer us a lot of compassion and kindness that was much needed. The sort of thing... there was just plain glass in the lavatory door and everyone could see you doing your business, which didn't appeal to me at all. We slept four in a bedroom and I don't know when or if ever the sheets were changed but none the less, in that very happy go lucky household there was a warmth that I hadn't found in the previous home and strangely enough for an untidy boy of fourteen I was much happier there than in the first place. That was in January 1941. The husband, the foster father, was a detective on the railway and was very much occupied during the war with escorting Royalty, and would often come home and tell us that he had escorted the king or Winston Churchill to some place or other on their private train.

In April 1941 there occurred what was the most upsetting traumatic two weeks of my life. One morning there was a letter arrived and it was in my father's hand and I... have no idea to this day why... but the moment I saw that letter I burst into tears. The letter was taken and read and my foster mother and strangely enough the mother of one of the other boys who happened to be visiting called me in and sat down with me and told me in the most loving terms that my mother had just died. That was Easter 1941, April 15th . She had some days before been taken ill with what they thought was flu, it turned out to be meningitis and she died on the Easter Tuesday and they were extremely kind to me, but goodness knows how I would have fared at the first home. Some friends from

Hastings came and took me over to Ware, in Hertfordshire, to see my sister Sylvia and we walked together on the 18<sup>th</sup> April, the day my mother was buried. Sylvia was called out of her class at the High School and she came out and stood in the waiting room and I remember her words, she simply said to me, "Poor mum."

Following that the... day of mum's funeral... the family I was living with thought it would be kind to take my mind off the things that had been happening to me, and decided to buy me a bicycle. I was very proud, because it had drop handle bars, which were very appealing, and I went out on the road without any warning or training to ride this bicycle. Ten days after my mother died on the 25<sup>th</sup> April at half past three in the afternoon I was coming down the hill to approach the house where I was living, at the central cross roads in St Albans, and the traffic lights said, "Stop" so I stopped. On my right was a London brick lorry, which had also stopped. He, which I did not observe indicated he was going to turn left, I wanted to go straight forward and when the lights changed we both did what we wanted to and I with my bicycle went under his wheels. My life was saved by the fact that... my bicycle fell on top of me and the lorry went over it, crushing me by transferred weight.... I still have a hole in my leg where the pedal went in and a scar on my head where I received serious injuries. My father was contacted and told that I probably wouldn't survive the night and he came up post haste from Hastings.

I was taken to the St Albans Hospital and spent six weeks there fortunately slowly getting better. When I regained consciousness some days after the accident, the Dean of St Albans Abbey was standing by my bedside saying a prayer, and told me that when I was dead he would pray for my soul. I hadn't realized that I was dying, so I decided that I wanted to live, and after I got better I went and called on him to thank him for coming to see me and he said to me, "God has given you your life back, what are you going to do with it?" That was the beginning of the trail that led me to become a priest.

1941 was a time of terrible 'goings on' in the war but like most people we tried to keep our little lives going on as normal and as soon as I had fully recovered I did a paper round and delivered a hundred and thirty papers in the morning before school. I joined the local Army Cadet Force and was kitted out in a uniform much too big for me, and remember distinctly being told I was a German paratrooper for all night manoeuvres at the Verulamium, where we were supposed to be hunted by the British soldiers. It seemed silly playing games when the real thing was happening on our very doorstep, but that's what happened. School went on apace and having been a teacher later in life, I realised how extremely difficult it must have been for the school staff to maintain any kind of cohesion to our studies and any sort of progress.

I know that both our parents saw my Grammar School education and my sister's as a golden opportunity, and I have a very happy memory of my mother putting her arms around me on the day a letter arrived saying I had passed the eleven plus examination. I knew that this opportunity should not be missed, whatever was going on in the world, and that at all costs our education should proceed, which it did, but life would never be as it was in the Grammar School before the war, it was a very hard existence. I felt when I first went to the Grammar School in 1938 that I hadn't known discipline like it. It was very rigid and you got the cane if you misbehaved. You were told to be in a certain place at a certain time and you had to be there. Although prefects didn't have the right to cane you, they had the right to discipline you and they gave out punishment drills or detentions 'ad lib'. We had a journal in which we had to keep a record of rewards and punishments. It was much harder in St Albans than being at the school in Hastings, because we had to work in all these different places and we were separated from our own home and we were living under extremely difficult conditions, in fact everyone was. The war impinged on our daily lives in hundreds of ways. There wasn't much food about, it was rationed: then there were the daily news bulletins, which we all sat in awed silence to hear every night at six o clock on the radio, it governed us even though we were growing children. In fact I often look at fourteen year olds and think, "What do you know?" They perhaps never wonder what is going on in the world at large but it was forced upon us, well on everyone! I remember seeing, for instance, during the Battle of Britain in the main streets of St Albans the big placards '179 German Planes Shot Down Today' and that sort of thing. The evidence of the war was all around us, but the school played an important part though, because I can still name almost every boy in my class, all mutual friends. I never got the cane at St Albans but I was hauled out to the front by my ear more than once. I took to that all right, it didn't worry me as I was a rather well behaved kind of child, I didn't get into any real naughtiness at school but all boys, particularly boys in their teenage years love being in gangs sometimes up to 'no good,' and out of school we would run about the streets together at night, freed from the discipline of school and war.

I can certainly see the difficult task the teachers had. Several of our staff had been subject to terrible things in the First War and the physics teacher became absolutely distraught one day during an experiment when some chlorine escaped from the tube and he rushed out of the room and slammed the door, because he had been gassed in the war. Our English teacher Conisby had been 'shell shocked' in the war and if any boy misbehaved he would just put his head in his hands and cry. Oh those teachers come back to me! The PE teacher was a very young man, what was his name? Donahue, or that's what we named him, after the Jockey Steve Donahue, a very flashing, dashing young man. He went off to the war and never came back. Our chemistry master was Tom Cookson, who married Catherine Cookson the novelist. In her life story there's much about Tom who died three weeks after she did, of a broken heart, but he taught us chemistry. I remember him particularly well, in fact, in recent years before he died he was on television with his wife and I could have recognised him anywhere.

At no time did we return to Hastings during those years. There was just one occasion before my mother died, when she did come on one very hurried journey to see us on a Green Line bus, first to St Albans, then to Ware on another bus and back to St Albans. I had a dreadful moment when I stood in the High Street and watched her get on the Green Line bus to go back home, and feeling my heart would break. In fact, had I but known it, that was the last time I was to ever see her. The effect of what happened to me, losing mother and nearly my own life in a fortnight played a very big part in the whole trauma of being evacuated.

It wasn't long after my accident that the kind lady with whom we lived suddenly took ill and died. She had pernicious anaemia, and she was taken to hospital and she was dead, so again the time came to move on. For a while I was sent to a Local Authority Evacuee Hostel for some six months, which was a very impersonal affair but because there were other boys and girls there in a similar plight, we had quite a lot of fun, as children make fun wherever they are, and we went off to school every morning from the Hostel and back again at night.

During all this time I only remember my mother's one visit before she died and my father coming when I had my accident. He came in the ten days between my accident and my mother's death as well but was obviously very upset himself. He stayed in the billet where I was for a couple of nights, but it was such a sad time, I can't remember much about what was said or done. Then he came up when I was so ill... but I don't know much about that. I have particular memories after recovering from my accident of getting a new bicycle which my uncle bought me and cycling over sixteen miles to Ware and back again to see my sister for the day and just walking around with her and seeing the family with whom she lived, and so on.

I was moved from the Hostel to another home and this time it was a very warm and comfortable home. The foster mother encouraged us to call her Queenie and they had a nice dog and it was a homely place. I was only there some months when once again there was some event. This time the ageing grandmother was coming out of hospital and had to have my room, so I had to go somewhere else and I really cannot remember where

I went for the last few months of my school life. However I took the School Certificate Examination sitting in the local Congregational School room, and somehow or other managed to achieve enough passes and credits to Matriculate. I then went into the sixth form at school but was only there for three weeks. I was so unhappy at school I thought I must try something else, whatever it is it can't be worse than this.

Following my mother's death my father remarried. He married a rather simple soul who'd had a disastrous life of her own. She was neglected and abused throughout her childhood but she herself had got a brother who coming from this very sad and difficult childhood home, had made good. He'd gone to London and become the Managing Director of a toothpaste firm and he made an offer to me and said, "You can either come and work for me and I'll teach you all I know about business, or you can have lodgings with me and find work elsewhere". I chose to work for him and find lodgings elsewhere, and on 29$^{th}$ September (I think it was 1943), I left St Albans and went to live in Acton, West London, and went to work on the Park Royal Industrial Estate.

My lodgings were with a Mr and Mrs Edmonds of Acton who had two sons. The youngest of them was a very handsome young man called Ernie. Ernie had just been across to Canada in the Royal Air Force to train as a navigator in the new two engine Mosquito aircraft. He came home for his 21$^{st}$ Birthday on which his engagement to be married was announced, and I was invited to join in the celebrations in that home, and Mary, his girl friend, played the piano. There was much fun and they even tried his parachute on me, being rather a small fellow it hung on me rather low. That was on Wednesday. He went back two days later, and on the following Monday the telegram arrived to say he'd been shot down and killed. I remember the heartbreak and the horror in that home the moment that telegram arrived. In fact those two parents were never the same again and shortly after they asked me to find other lodgings because they couldn't cope with their grief as well as me.

When it came to my seventeenth birthday in November 1943 my sister Sylvia visited me in Acton, she was then fifteen.

Then it was my turn to

register for National Service in November 1944 on my eighteenth birthday I went for a medical at Edgware Drill Hall and the medical officer looked at me and said, "Is that all there is?" And he said, "Take your jacket off again, laddie!" and he walked all the way round me and said, "There's not enough of you!" I had volunteered for the navy, but they wouldn't accept me because I was made grade 4. He said, "Read that chart", because I had bad eyesight. And I said, "What chart?" And he said, "Are you trying to be funny?" And so he sent me to a specialist in Harley Street, who sent back a report on the condition of my eyes and that together with my size made me grade 4 but I remember that I was of the age group when we became eighteen in 1944 we went immediately into National Service and a number of my friends didn't come back, like poor Ernie.

While I was there in London it was the time of the doodlebugs. That's the pilotless bomber aircraft that came across and exploded haphazardly over London during the months of May and June 1944. We would spend the night in the Anderson shelter in the garden, and come up each morning to find the garden littered with shrapnel, more from our own anti-aircraft guns than from anything from the doodlebugs. On one particular occasion in the office, as the office boy, when the aircraft imminent warning went, I had to carry all the young girls' typewriters down to the long concrete air raid shelter. One day the imminent went as the aircraft came overhead and it exploded so close nearby that I was blown down the stairs of the air raid shelter, clutching a typewriter. I remember picking myself off the floor thinking, "What was all that about?"

I had already taken various business examinations and incidentally I took

part one RSA Book Keeping at Chiswick Polytechnic in the first week in June 1944. That was the week of D-Day and the day after I sat that exam, Chiswick Polytechnic was hit by a flying bomb and destroyed. But I went on making what effort I could by going to evening classes three or four nights a week because our little lives seemed to go on almost as though the war wasn't happening although it affected us in so many ways. On June 6th 1944 I went to the local opticians to have my eyes tested. To me the most important matter of that day was not the fact that the great invasion had taken place, but that I was told because I had extremely poor eyesight never to marry a girl with glasses.

Another memory, though nothing to do with the war as such, was the time of the London pea souper fogs and the great horror of coming out of Acton Underground Station, with which I was so familiar, and not knowing where I was... not knowing whether I was in the road or on the pavement, whether I should turn left or right and feeling totally lost in a very thick pea souper. I stayed working at the toothpaste firm, where I learned a lot about business, until very nearly the end of the war in 1945. Living in London I was no less lonely than I was in St Albans. In fact I used to pass my time at the weekends going about on tube trains, just looking in shop windows. Incidentally, going back to St Albans I particularly remember Christmas Day 1942. I spent that Christmas morning walking round the empty streets looking in shop windows and I swore to myself if ever I had a family of my own they would never have to walk around empty streets on Christmas Day. But back to my time in London, it was as I say still very lonely.

I already mentioned I was a choirboy so I thought perhaps I might find friendship at the local church. I went to St Gabrielle's Acton on several occasions and nobody ever said, "Good Day" to me or asked who I was. I even saw a notice that said there was an evening youth club, so I went to it and sat there and nobody spoke to me, so I didn't go any more. It wasn't until much later in my early twenties that I felt called to the Christian ministry myself but that is another story.

It was such a lonely time in London and by 1945 my sister had returned to Hastings and several of my friends, so I went down for one or two weekends and felt heartbroken every time I went back. I decided that for better or worse I would have to leave London and find work in Hastings. I found a very monotonous job in the local building society, which was not far removed from a Dickension environment, because I sat on a three-legged stool making entries in leather-bound ledgers all day. I was there for some eighteen months.

The war ended in Europe on 8th May 1945 after my return home, and I particularly remember standing with the friends I had rediscovered in Hastings town centre at 3 o'clock that afternoon, and hearing the voice of Churchill relayed on loud speakers telling us all that the war was over. We walked about and there was dancing in the streets and it was a wonderful time and we stayed up all night, it has very wonderful memories. My sister by this time was a telephone operator in the local Post Office and when her time of duty was over we trooped off to meet her, and I don't think I'd ever seen her so excited as she was telling us that everybody had rung everybody else that day and there had never been so many phone calls made.

So the war came to an end, but life was still pretty hard in many ways. Locally, great dragon's teeth, concrete dragon's teeth, were all the way along the front. The pier had been blown into two and everywhere there were rolls and rolls of barbed wire. It took a long time to get back to anything like normal, and the winter of 1947 was possibly the coldest I can ever remember, and there were power cuts and no heating. By this time I was working in a concrete office at Rye Harbour where there was no heating in very arctic conditions indeed.

Geographically, I've always felt that Hastings was my home because I'd always loved the environment of the West Hill and the East Hill and walking miles with friends, and I loved the countryside. So geographically Hastings was home but domestically, when we went back and mum had died and we had to live with my father and stepmother, I could never call that home, it was just a place where I had to live. When we returned to Hastings after the war, we went back to extremely painful and sordid circumstances, in which my father and stepmother lived, and it is a time that I choose rather to forget than remember. So it wasn't until I got married and settled down as a married person that I had my own home. I now have five children and eight grandchildren and have been married for forty-five years, but I carry with me, as we all do, the inheritance of my childhood.

The effect of my war on me, as for many young people, was pretty profound, most of all I feel that we had no youth. I see my children and my grandchildren growing up, living in comparative prosperity with money to spend and the opportunity to enjoy the growing years of their lives; able to educate themselves, go to University, do all the things that were so very difficult for us to achieve. We've often felt when we look at our children and our grandchildren that we missed out on our youth. Of course, it would have been sour grapes to mention it, because one only has to look across to the Continent and think that there were millions of Jewish children who not only missed out on their youth but were gassed and lost their lives. Or I think of the young men in my school who never came back from the war. The boy who sat next to me in my class in 1938 was married and three weeks later was killed in the war. Several boys I knew never came back so it would be, as I say, sour grapes to make much of it, but the truth is that we did not have a very enjoyable youth: it was mortgaged to war.

I feel still that we lost out, that our growing up was inhibited by the war, and I don't believe that I matured as I should have done had I grown up in happier circumstances, until many years later. Yes, it changed my life entirely. There is one particular occasion I can remember when I went into a park in St Albans, I don't know what year it was even, but as I sat down on the grass with my bike flung down beside me, I made a vow aloud and promised myself that whatever it cost I would improve myself and would make something of my life, and that if I got married and had children, they would never have the kind of childhood that I had.

One wonders what our future would have been had there been no war? Who can tell? It may be that in some twisted way it was the war that gave us the opportunity to break away from the poverty of our childhood, but at a cost of such loneliness and heartache that one would hardly choose to go that way. To end on a happier note, at Hastings after the war we rediscovered our local church, which had an enthusiastic new vicar. He got together all the young people returning from the war and formed us into a group, and created a fellowship that laid the foundations of my wanting to become a priest. Having said that the Dean, of the Abbey at St Albans who came to see me in hospital when I was thought to be dying, later invited me to be prepared for Confirmation and on 11th December 1941 I was confirmed in the Abbey and became a member of The Server's Guild and served at the high altar. It was then I began to feel the influence, the Christian influence, which provided some reassurance in my sad and lonely childhood.

I haven't gone into the spiritual implications of becoming a priest. It's certainly something to do with the fact that one believes that God is a God of love, and that through Him we are able to share love with those who need it. My philosophy of life was affected by the emotional feeling world of those days and I was aware of the coldness and the 'cut-offness'... very much so. What happened to me was that at a very formative prepubescent time of my life the one source of love that was my mother had been cut off. Of course once I became a priest that was intellectualised and reasoned out, I mean one hardly operates solely on the emotional level, but the thought, feeling and will all come into it. Obviously what I look for in my own life is the warmth that was lacking for me during the war in relationships and want to make sure that others get that especially my own children, I never want them ever to be lonely. The most important thing that parents can offer to their children is warmth and love.

## Chapter 5. 'The betrayal was the thing... by many... including the authorities.'

### Sylvia's Story (sister to Keith).

I was born in 1928 in Hastings into a poor family, and at that time my father was working as a cook on Pullman trains. My brother was born two years before me. He was a pyloric baby, which meant that he had a muscular obstruction at the entrance to his stomach and spent a lot of time in and out of hospital in his early life, but there wasn't much wrong with me when I came along. We had a difficult life because my father drank too much at times, what would now be called 'going on a binge'. He was a sailor before his marriage, and had run away to sea from an unhappy home life when he was fourteen, but had left the navy to be with my mother.

Most of the time he was a marvellous father, he repaired our shoes on a shaped iron last which I still have, and he could turn basic ingredients into a gourmet meal. He would help my mother with the washing, I can still see him with his shirtsleeves rolled back and up to his elbows in soapsuds, but when he had a drinking session it was as though he was bent on the destruction of himself and all of us, as he used the hard earned money needed for our survival. We were living in rented rooms and one of my earliest memories is of a first floor flat that we were thrown out of because he fell on the stairs one night when he was drunk. The landlady who lived downstairs was a devout Salvationist and she was very good to us most of the time but this proved too much for her and she evicted us. We went to a ground floor flat next time and I was very happy there because we had our first kitten, the little thing captivated me as many subsequent pussies have ever since. I was happy as a child, but very aware that there was a problem over which no one seemed to have any control.

I started school when I was three, because my mother needed to go to work and I can vaguely remember the Infants' school, where we went to bed for a rest on little low beds in the afternoons. I was very happy at Mount Pleasant Primary school, although the discipline was extremely strict. The headmaster Mr Hopkins would line the boys up in his office when they had done something that he thought wasn't quite right and cane them. The naughty girls would line up with them and watch the boys being caned on their hands but he never ever caned a girl, he just told them off, I didn't think too much about the boys but even they seemed to respect him because it didn't seem like unfair punishment. Apart from that he was a great innovator. For instance, he introduced us to the telephone because none of us had one at home in those days. One was installed in every classroom and each day a child was chosen to phone his office, so that from very early on we need have no fear of it. I just remember being happy at that school and having friends.

Being attached to the church and Sunday school made up our social life  and the teachers took us on an annual outing, but that was about it. As I got older I became my mother's friend and companion. She was a cinema cleaner, starting work at eight in the morning, but was always home by early afternoon when we came out of school. She had to work on Saturday mornings and would take me with her to listen to the man practisng on his Wurlitzer organ, while she cleaned the cinema, and sometimes I helped her out. There were no Hoovers in those days, the seats were all cleaned with a dustpan and brush, and there was no protection from picking up the odd flea. Once one attached itself to you it was not easy to get rid of, the most effective way was by drowning, and even then, given half a chance, the flea would make every attempt to drag its soggy body up the side of the receptacle. As well as meeting the occasional flea I got to know mum's boss, the lady who was in charge of the cinema, and she was always very kind to me, she admired my auburn hair and told me that many women would pay a great deal of money to have hair that colour. She also gave my mother two free cinema tickets a week, and if the film was suitable mum chose me to go with her and that became a great interest, because of course there was no television in those days and we were too poor to own a radio. Every Sunday morning after Sunday school I went out for a walk with my dad and he always took me down the town. My mother persuaded me to go even if I didn't want to because she was trying to delay his going to the pub. He would walk round with me and buy me sweets, usually hard chocolate caramels and then send me home on my own while he stayed in the town and had his drink, but I didn't ever tell her that he would leave me in a passage with lemonade and sweets, and drink while I was still with him. I loved going out with him, though, because sometimes we went to see friends of his, who had big collections of cigarette cards that I could look at but we could never afford to go on holiday or anything like that. I only remember going away once with

52

them and that was at Christmas when we went up to London in a coach to see my uncle and our cousins, and for the first time I saw a Christmas tree.

It sounds as though we didn't have much, but Hastings was a great place to live. Dad and mum taught us to swim in the sea and the town had a rhythm of its own as summer visitors came and went. I resented their arrival, because we lived near a greensward where there were see-saws and swings and roundabouts and I used to think I owned them because I could run down there whenever I liked. But when the summer visitors came the swings were full, and I objected to having to stand there and wait for all those strange kids before it was my turn, and I made that quite obvious at times. I enjoyed the place being more deserted in the winter but it always seemed bitterly cold and my hands and feet were covered in chilblains. My mother used to send me out if it snowed with any stale bread for the seagulls, she couldn't resist their cries as they came inland for food.

Another happy memory was the annual Carnival. My mother used to borrow costumes from the lady she worked for and dress me up and take me into the parade, I remember going as a penguin and collecting money for the hospital in a bucket and being very proud of my mum making this contribution. She was deeply involved with the church, in that she went regularly on Sundays. In the morning I'd be sent to Sunday school then down to the town with my father and in the evening I would go to church with my mother and my brother Keith who was in the choir. I used to have a wonderful time with him as well. We were street children and near us there was a place where cars were garaged, but in those days there were more garages than cars, it was a safe place to play. He used to put on shows and wear an old battered top hat he'd found, and we'd get boxes and turn them upside down, and charge the children a halfpenny to come and sit on them and see the performance. Keith was two years older than me and I was very proud of him. I had my own friends, of course, but crowds of us would often play in the same place. He could be quite a dare devil really and took me on the cliffs nearby where we were forbidden to go and I can remember being quite terrified trying to climb them. He had an air gun and used to take me out with that which was also forbidden. I remember going out in the snow with him making an enormous snowball much bigger than myself and we had fun together whatever the weather, and so much freedom.

The first thing I remember about the threat of war was being in the cinema with my mother and watching the Pathe News showing the negotiations with Mr Chamberlain and understanding something of the seriousness of the situation. The film was 'Stagecoach', it was good but as it went on I lost interest and began to get extremely anxious. I was overwhelmed with this feeling that something terrible was going to happen and I pleaded with my mother, "Take me home, mummy, take me home," but she was enjoying the film and couldn't understand what was the matter with me, she didn't realise how frightened I had become and asked me if she could see, "A bit more and a little bit more." I can't remember whether she did take me home before it ended or not, but hope she didn't in a way because she had so few pleasures to come.

I saw the London evacuees arrive in Hastings. I was playing with a yo-yo whilst sitting on the top of a small pillar by the front porch of our house. I often used to sit there and on this occasion my mother was on the steps talking to a neighbour when we saw this crocodile of weary children straggling along on the other side of the road. Her heart went out to them, "Poor little children, poor little children!" and I said, "Why are they poor little children mum?" and she said, "Because they have had to leave their mummies and their daddies and come away from London". I can see them now but I just went on playing with my yo-yo. We didn't take an evacuee. We had no room, we only had two bedrooms, I had one and

my parents the other and my brother had to sleep in the room we called the front room, his bed and the sofa were in there and we covered his bed up and used it as a living room during the daytime. My mother's parents had left London at the threat of war and were coming to stay with us for a while but I don't know where they slept.

I was ten years old when war was declared on the Sunday morning of the 3rd of September 1939 and I became eleven two days later on 5th September. I had attended Sunday school at 10 0'clock and then gone to a friend's house on that particular morning, and I heard Mr Chamberlain's speech on her radio so I ran home just before the air raid warning went. My mother was leaving the house to go to the local shop that was open on Sunday mornings, where we were given 'tick', which meant everything was put in 'the book' until the next Friday pay day. Mum seemed to take no notice of the fact that the siren had sounded and we walked down together. The street suddenly became deserted and a woman leaned out of her window and screamed for a dog in the street to be taken in, and I looked at my mother and thought, "Why has the dog got to be taken in and we're outside?" But she said, "There's no need for that, there's nothing happening" and that influenced me for the rest of the war, the idea that if nothing was happening it was all right, there was no need to panic.

A couple of days after the announcement of war, round about my birthday time, I'd gone up from primary into the High School because I'd passed the scholarship, the eleven plus, so I was awarded a free place but unfortunately none of my close friends came with me, they had gone to the Central School. I didn't like the High School very much because my parents couldn't afford the uniform and the first thing that happened on the first day was that one of the girls said, "You've got the wrong colour coat on". From the moment she said that I thought, "You're all a lot of snobs" and felt different. When I passed the scholarship I was given a clothing grant by the Education Authority but my brother didn't have enough in his grant to buy the school blazer and had already been at the Grammar School for a year, so my mother begged me to let him have his mauve blazer but then I couldn't have the right uniform. There were a certain percentage of scholarship children amongst the privately paid children but the friends I made all seemed to be very rich. One of the girls had had her hair permed, and I remember being incredulous that any one could afford it or that anyone would want to and it confirmed for me that they were all snobs but I must admit I couldn't differentiate who was a scholarship child and who wasn't, except myself and when I had my coat on I felt I stuck out like a sore thumb. Although I felt a bit of an outsider I was absolutely stimulated at the same time, because at home we hadn't any books or even an accumulator radio (or wireless as it was called then). The main source of light was an oil lamp on the table until one gas jet was inserted in the living room, otherwise we used candles; but the whole ethos and atmosphere of the school captivated me, and for that I loved it. I was so interested in everything that was going on, but at the same time I felt ashamed of my poverty, and didn't quite know whether I was one of them or not, and yet I felt that I had a right to be there. Keith was fine at the Grammar School and we had already lost a lot of contact because he had became deeply involved with his school and homework and as I moved up I became deeply involved with mine; we were no longer happy-go-lucky street kids.

Meantime the war was progressing, and down on the sea front huge tank traps and rolls of barbed wire had appeared. We were down there one day when a crowd gathered on the beach and I couldn't see what they were looking at, so Keith and I ran off. We tunnelled through the barbed wire and he helped me to climb on to a tank trap where I stood very briefly and saw men in boats coming back from Dunkirk, but by this time my mother had come after us and I can remember her arms lifting me down and blood, where we had been torn on the barbed wire, so she took us to a chemist nearby. He put plasters on us and I said, "I want to go back" because I couldn't understand what was happening and it all seemed exciting but of course she wouldn't hear of it as she attempted to protect us from the ravages of war. A few days later we were told there was going to be an invasion. I didn't see the going of them but the London evacuees had disappeared, some had been sharing our school, so I knew they had gone.

I was still feeling the loss of all my old friends at the primary school and although I'd started to make new ones these relationships were still in their infancy when we were told that we ourselves were being sent away, it was our turn to become evacuees, if we didn't go we would have no schooling. I know now it was said to be a choice, but as far as we were concerned choice didn't come into it. My father was unusual for his day and age, because there were girls passing the scholarship who were not sent to the High School because their parents felt that girls didn't need a higher standard of education but my father said when I passed that his daughter would be treated the same as his son. He wanted me to have the right to be educated; he was extremely keen on it. He was always educating himself, and although we had no books he would use the library avidly, and he was dedicated to us getting out of the poverty trap and into professions. So that is why it felt right for me to be there and there was no question of not being evacuated if we were going to lose that right, his views on education were vital to him and us, so he was left with no choice but to send us away.

It all happened on 21st July 1940 and I remember getting up in the morning but I can't remember my brother going at all; he just wasn't there. Whether he didn't say goodbye to me I just don't know, but as my father left to go to work I ran out into the street after him although he had already kissed me goodbye, and he hugged me and kissed me again and then said, "Well don't let's make a meal of it" and turned round and walked along the street and I still stood there: but he never looked back. I've never forgotten that; that he didn't look back. My mother and grandfather saw me off amongst all the other parents who were collecting in the town centre where the whole of Hastings children seemed to be evacuating on that same day. When I said goodbye to my mum I remember my grandfather saying, "Just let her go gal, let her go," because she hugged me to her, reluctant to let go when it came to it. Then we were on this bus and looking out of the window and waving to our parents all standing there because they weren't allowed to come to the station. I can't remember getting on to the train but I remember being on it very vividly.

I associated evacuation with education and imminent invasion, creating this feeling that something terrible was going to happen at any minute. The Germans were expected to come across the Channel, and they were said to be very close. My brother had been told at school that when the Germans came they were not to worry their parents but conform to whatever they were told to do, and they were not to make a fuss about anything because it would add to the problems. The whole atmosphere was, "You've got to get out and you've got to get out quickly," which is exactly what we were doing.

Our particular lot were in one of those carriages with tables in between us with the French teacher to keep us company. I was excited when we first started, feeling that I was going out into the world, because Hastings had been my whole environment up to then, but it wore off quickly. We went through London without stopping and I can remember a woman with a baby in her arms waving to us from her garden as we went through. Then suddenly like when I was in the pictures with my mum I got this kind of premonition of disaster. I couldn't tell what it seemed to be around, just a sudden overwhelming fear of disaster and I put my arms on the table resting my head down on them and shut my eyes. The French mistress's voice said, "Don't wake her, let her sleep". But I wasn't asleep, I had just become totally terrified on that train, perhaps because I had some understanding of what was really happening and felt I needed to hide that fear from the others. We didn't know where we were after leaving London behind because all the station names had been removed and had no idea how long the journey would be, but now I've no recall of how long it seemed or of getting off the train in Ware in Hertfordshire, where we were walked round to the school which we were going to attend just near the station. Now I was part of that crocodile of children and it was my mum who wasn't there for me.

We must have stood around in that hall some time before six of us were taken off in a car by a harassed lady who remains faceless. I asked a girl called Margaret, with whom I had started a friendly relationship, to come with me. My brother had gone to a different town altogether with his school and I begged Margaret to stay with me because I was frightened and lonely, but she wanted to anyway. She was the only child of elderly parents, a plump sort of girl, and I somehow felt a bit safe with her. We got into this car together with four other girls and were taken to a council estate where the faceless lady told us to get out of the car and stand against a wall while she took two of the girls off and said, "Wait here". So the four of us stood against this high wall in total silence while she marched off with the other two, we never spoke and it seemed gloomy as the early evening came on.

When she came back the lady took Margaret and me off and left the other two by the wall. She walked us on to this huge council estate and left us at number four. When we went into this house a meal was ready and it was very clean and tidy, and a middle-aged couple lived there who had never had any children. I remember looking at this table all set ready for us with salad, which I'd hardly ever eaten in my life, because we couldn't afford it I suppose and thinking it was cold and I didn't want it but I sort of picked at it and then we were put into a double bed together. The minute I got into bed, I sat up and said to Margaret, "I'm now going to plan how to get home. Tomorrow we're running away. After breakfast we're leaving here and we're going away, we're going home". She thought this was a great idea, so we went right on planning this escape until we fell asleep but when we got up in the morning my foster father was waiting for us and he said, "When you'd gone to bed last night I sat on the stairs and heard every word, and you're not running away." So that scotched that one. He wasn't angry, but he was quite firm and he turned out to be a kind man. To get to school that morning it was a long, long walk and all the other girls were there in the hall again. They all seemed subdued and some were crying because they hadn't had enough to eat and seemed very unhappy, and others were OK. Strangely enough I just recall registering what other people were feeling and nothing about myself.

We stayed at our billet for two weeks. Aunty and uncle as we called them were kind, but it seemed dull, as though the bottom had fallen out of the world. Aunty tried to cherish us in her way but I didn't feel free, I knew I'd got to be good. I knew the first thing we had to do was to write to our parents so that they knew where we were living. I wrote a letter and my mother wrote back and said she was so pleased we were all right, but I didn't feel I was all right in some ways. Years later a friend who had not been evacuated told me that mum wasn't all right either. She had been unable to go to work after we went for a while, and the day after we left had run round to her house with a beautiful red apple saying she had to give it to her because she couldn't give it to me. After two weeks my foster mother said she'd had a letter from the hospital. She'd been on a waiting list for an operation so she could no longer look after us, but she would have us back when she came out of hospital and was better. Now she knew that all the billets were full up, I suppose, because she said, "We've got to find somewhere for you to live," and took us out into the street. We were at number four in this long, long road and she knocked on all the doors, one after the other, every door in the street and every single person said, "No". Some of them were quite blasphemous about it and I can remember saying to her, "Ooh, don't leave us there aunty, don't leave us there," when we were met with a tirade of verbal abuse from a woman leaning out of an upstairs window. Then when we thought no one was going to take us in eventually we got to number 104 where a man who was standing at the garden gate called out to his wife who was standing at the front door, "Shall we take these two kids then?" And she replied, "Why not?" So aunty just handed us over. I don't remember going back for any possessions or anything, we just went in and that of course was a totally different ball game; another world.

This couple were 'East Enders' from Bow in London, they'd been sent down to Ware on a scheme for re-housing or rehabilitating the slums and had one son who was younger than me. They spoke rhyming slang so half the time I didn't know what they were talking about. I didn't know that the 'apples and pears' were stairs and your 'uncle Ned' was your head or the 'trouble and strife' was your wife. They didn't believe in education, they didn't believe in God, and they were not just talking rhyming slang but to my uninitiated ears were extremely blasphemous, every other word was 'bloody' this or something that and as I'd not heard anybody speak like that in my whole life before I can still remember the kind of shock of having to adapt but I learnt rhyming slang extremely quickly, so that I could follow the conversation, but I didn't swear because that seemed to me not what I should be doing.
Now there was this boy there and I thought, "Ooh, I've got another brother" but at the end of the two weeks my first foster mother came out of hospital and Margaret said, "I'm going back" but I didn't think I wanted to. I had to write to my mother so that she was fully aware of what was going on and she insisted that I would go and see this lady. Instead of that, because I was deciding not to go back, I used to duck down when we had to pass her house on the way to school and walk under the hedge, so that she couldn't see me, because I felt I was doing something wrong by I wanting to stay where I was. My mother was upset by all this and tried to organise it all from a distance and said in her letters, "If you don't go back, I want you to go and see the lady and let me know how she is" and so on and so on, but she didn't come on the bus laid on by Maidstone & District from Hastings. I knew that was because she couldn't afford it or take time off work or leave my father or her

parents but we had lots of correspondence; I've still got her letters. I stayed but didn't know what was happening to me, I was being drawn into this family, into an enclosed sort of world.

In the end I stayed with them for four and a half years and they drew me into their world, cutting me off, wanting me to become one of them. They were invaded by other members of their family from the East End of London because of the bombing, and various people kept arriving. Another evacuee, Sally, arrived too when Margaret went, and I had to share my bed again. This time it was a single ironed framed bed and as Margaret and Sally were both fatter than me I spent half the night on the iron frame, so I was quite pleased when Margaret went back to the other house, and the other girl Sally who came didn't stay either, she couldn't take it and went back home. But I didn't have it all to myself, any young children in the host family that came and needed a bed would share mine so I had to get used to it. The room was absolutely basic, it had no light and I would read by sitting on the windowsill and leaning out of the window catching the last of the evening light. I can't remember a single picture, I can't remember any ornament; it was so basic, the box room I suppose really.

My foster parents own son was quite a bit younger than me but I was expected to play with him and I was always being sent off upstairs where they'd converted a room into a kind of playroom and I was expected to do a lot of housework and chores as well. My foster father was a stoker on a 'puffer train' and started each day from Stratford main line station in London. When the Blitz was going on we could see London burning from the front gate and my foster mother would stand out there and wait for him to see if he was ever coming home. When he did come back he was all black from the coal, and where he'd had to stop the train and get off to put incendiary bombs out with his tin hat, as the German planes followed the train. They could follow the trains along the tracks because of the fire and smoke from the engines, which was impossible to hide. If you dropped a tin hat on incendiaries the lack of oxygen would extinguish the flame.

My mother kept talking about coming down and whether we should go home for Christmas in her letters and then my father found himself 'on the dole'. He had lost his job as a cook on Pullman trains years ago, because drink was too available on the train and at stations, and was at that time a bus conductor but there was nobody left to ride on the buses, so he got the sack. Because he had no work, mum had to go on working to hold everything together, and this meant she had to clean the cinema at weekends. I think there was money sent to my foster mother from mum for various things, and she sent me clothes and a bit of pocket money.

Mum wrote and said that she couldn't come and fetch us for Christmas, because she would have to cross London and take us back and she couldn't afford to do that, and asked me to pray for work for my father. I knew what it meant because I'd lived at home when he had lost his work before, but I was angry because most of my friends went back for Christmas.

This first Christmas away from home was different to anything I had ever known. It was noisy, they played cards and they taught me to play Whist, which I picked up very quickly because they played for halfpennies and pennies and I needed to win what seemed quite a lot of money to me at the time, and they dubbed me as a 'card sharper' from the beginning.

My father solved the employment problem by doing his bit for the country and joining the AFS, (the Auxiliary Fire Service), which later became the National Fire Service. This meant he had to live on the station for two nights out of every three to be on call during the air raids. They didn't just put the fires out they had to help dig the people out as well, but he was being paid again and my mother kept promising to come; then one day she did come. First she went to St Albans on the Maidstone & District bus to see my brother; then brought him over on another bus to see me for a short time. I hadn't seen any of my family from July 1940 and this was between January and Easter 1941, I can't remember the date but I know I waited for her all day and when I saw her coming up the long road, I ran like the wind to meet her and saw her brace herself to withstand the impact as I threw myself at her. After a long tight cuddle my tongue was loosed and I couldn't stop talking as I held on to her and we made our way to my foster home, where she spent about two hours with me and my foster mother. I remember her sitting there with my brother, eating her own sandwiches that she had brought with her and aunty saying to me, "Why don't you run outside and play with R-?" which I cannot understand to this day but my mother stretched out her hand and said, "No, you come and sit by me Syl-Syl", which is what she called me and she said to aunty, "She wants to stay with me".

I went to see her off on the bus back to St Albans with Keith. We'd left it to the last minute and it was a long walk and as we approached the bus stop, we saw that the bus was already there, and they had to run to catch it. They jumped aboard and made their way to the back of the bus and put the palms of their hands flat on the glass of the back window because there had been no time to kiss me goodbye and as the bus went away I watched my mother's hands and face disappear out of my life, it was the last time I was ever to see her, but of course I didn't know that at the time.

She wrote and said that she was sorry that they nearly missed the bus and she had to go away so quickly without having time to say goodbye and "It would be my turn next time." She would come to me first and "It would be great."

Copied from Sylvia's original letters from her mother

Hastings
Sussex.

My Dear S

Thank you for your letter dear, & I think mine must have crossed – but I hope you got it safely. I was glad to see my little girl once again, but oh! what a short visit, but after I have bought you both one or two things you

The next major event to occur was my twelfth birthday, made meaningful by a loving letter from mum and a parcel of small things that she could afford. It proved to be a particular milestone because soon after that I became a woman physically but I didn't go to my foster mother because I felt she was a hard woman, but years later had more understanding of the hard time she herself was having, because at that time her own son was suffering from measles and my foster father's sister, (still just called Sis) had come to us to escape from the bombing in London and was staying there with her little child of two Alice and her husband Mitch. I went to aunt Sis, who was also ill and confined to her bed with pleurisy; my foster mother had been making big grey poultices and putting them on her chest to ease the pain. It was early in the morning and she was sitting up when I went and stood by her but didn't need to say anything. She reached out to me realising what the trouble was, but with the effort and the intake of breath she screamed loudly with the pain, and I couldn't tell her what was the matter with me, and she couldn't speak. I thought she was going to die because she was taken with this terrible pain, in those days there were no antibiotics, no quick cures. My foster mother came running upstairs and dealt with it all, she showed me what to do and put a poultice on aunt Sis. This was my dramatic introduction to the menarche, I didn't know what it was and I wasn't sure what was happening to me; at the same time I was terrified because I thought aunt Sis was going to die but she did recover although she was very, very ill. Again it was my mother who reassured me when she wrote by telling me I was "preparing to be a beautiful lady" and how pleased she was to hear that the family were recovering from their illnesses.

The letters kept coming from mum, and now that my father was earning again they contained a promise "You are coming home for Easter, this time we'll arrange that you do come home for Easter." There had been no predicted invasion but the bombing was increasing because the German planes were being pushed back by the defence system in London. They were dropping their load before they left the coast, and also German pilots were practising bombing on the edge of England and going back. My foster mother had got into a way of demanding to read my mother's letters although she herself had letters from her, which I never saw. She probably wanted to check up what may be being said, and I was getting into a state of thinking, "No, you are not going to read mine". Then I received one from mum to say that they had had a terrible air raid, but they were all right and I felt it was very private and I wouldn't give aunty the letter. We were sitting in the living room in front of the black range and I tore the letter into tiny pieces and burnt it in front of her face and she said, "What did you do that for?" I've never forgotten destroying that letter because it was the last one I ever had in which my mother revealed for the first time what it was like to be in the bombing and asking me to pray for her. Years later I found out that she had been blown across Robertson Street as she left the cinema but was apparently uninjured.

About two weeks later a letter dropped on the mat and I ran and picked it up and saw it was from my father addressed to aunty and as I handed it over I said to myself, "My mum's dead". I said it silently, not to them but inside myself, and that turned out to be true. Aunty took the letter and whistled and walked off with it upstairs. Aunt Sis followed my foster mother up the stairs, and I thought, "I have to go up". I remember climbing those stairs but I can't remember which one told me, but aunt Sis put her arms around me and I started to cry and couldn't stop. It wasn't just an ordinary bout of crying, it was a terrible wild wailing that seemed to be coming from someone else, I can hear now but it eventually

63

stopped and I went downstairs. They said, "You needn't go to school today". There was a lodger in the house as well called Mr J-, who lived in the room that would have been their parlour and he had a rocking chair, and they let me sit in this rocking chair on that day. After the great bout of crying upstairs I can't remember making any noise but little Alice was playing on the floor near the rocking chair and she said, "It's raining in the house mummy" as she felt my tears falling on her silently. The next day I was sent to school. It was a sunny day and we were having lessons in the garden. We had lessons all over the place, in church halls, in churches, in the beautiful school garden if we were able and again it was the French mistress in charge. She must have known because she never said anything when I suddenly moved away from the class and sat on a step because I didn't feel I could stay with the others. She did ask one of the girls to come and sit with me and we sat there together in complete silence. Not one teacher spoke to me about my loss, not one teacher had anything to say at all.

My foster father wasn't there when the letter came but when he did come home aunty told him when we were all walking through the town. I was walking behind them and he turned round to me and said, "Cheer yourself up". I stopped walking and fell back and knew that somehow I'd got to be cheerful. Years later I found an old diary dated 1941, where I had recorded a fleeting visit from my father. I hadn't seen him since the day I originally left Hastings and can only imagine the enormous emotions that took the memory of that visit away.

Again I was in the town with my foster parents, ten days after my mother's death when I saw this person walking towards us a long way off and I said, "That's my father". They said, "He's come to see you again because your mother has died' and I said, "No, he hasn't, he's come to see me because something else has happened" and they said, "Don't be silly, don't be silly".

I ran towards him feeling pleased to see him and terrified at the same time. The police had sent for him because my brother had gone into the town on a bike and had an accident, he had been run over by a lorry and wasn't expected to live through the night. He said, "I've come to take you to see your brother before he dies." I remember going into the hospital in St Albans and sitting on the bed. I'd only seen my brother once and that was when he came that time with my mother. There was blood in the whites of his eyes, and because I wanted him to live I tried to feed him. My uncle was there, my mother's brother, and he took my father and me to a teashop when we came out of the hospital and I remember seeing these cakes on a cake stand but I couldn't eat one. Then my father took me back to Ware or my uncle, I don't remember which and they just left me in my foster home, my father left me; he didn't stay a single night because presumably he had to get back to the Fire Station. We had no telephones and I was quite sure that my brother was going to die because I'd been told that I'd been taken to see him before he died. I went to school as though nothing had happened but if someone mentioned their own mothers or my mother, I got this terrible stomach pain and could hardly stand up straight and decided it was better if nobody spoke to me.

I knew the river Lea was very dangerous; I'd heard about a blind man who had recently fallen in and drowned because the long trailing weeds held him under the water. I went along the towpath one day instead of going home, because all I wanted was to find my mother and as I thought my brother and if I died too they'd be there. It was a dull cloudy sort of day and I hurried to get out of sight of the town because you could see along the towpath from the bridge, and when I found a hidden area I knelt down and looked into the water. There was nobody there but the sun came out just at that moment and it shone on this quiet stretch of water where I was kneeling and showed me some sticklebacks darting about. I jumped up and started running and I just ran and ran and ran because I knew somehow that in spite of everything I wanted to live, that I didn't want to kill myself, and as I ran my foster brother came into my head and I wanted to tell him to bring his little net and catch some fishes.

Sometime after that my brother wrote to me to tell me that he had survived, I've still got the letter to say that he was recovering.

Keith's original letter to Sylvia from hospital

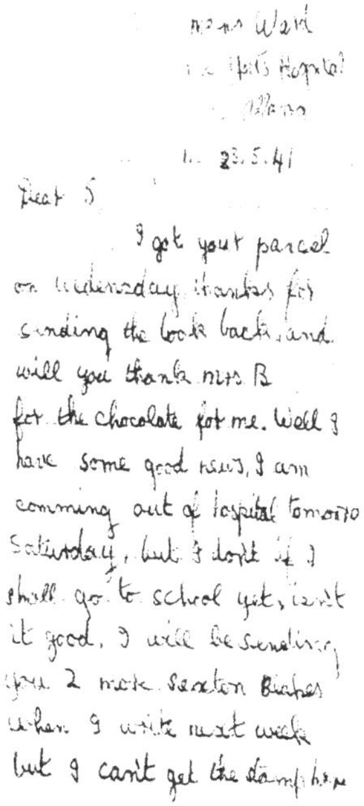

*[handwritten letter, partly illegible]*

Neen Ward
... this Hospital
... ...
... 23.5.41

Dear S

I got your parcel on Wednesday thanks for sending the book back, and will you thank nurse B for the chocolate for me. Well I have some good news, I am comming out of hospital tomorrow Saturday, but I don't if I shall go to school yet, isn't it good. I will be sending you 2 more Saxton Bishes when I write next week but I can't get the stamps here

you will have to wait till the next time. I will. Yesterday was raining day and I had Mrs Woodley and Brian, and that lady and man who saw my accident. Hope you are getting on O.K at school and hope you are keeping well, I am fine now, but still not too sure on my feet. When you answer this letter don't forget to address it to 32. Holywell the ... keep smiling

xx xx Your ever loving brother
xxx xxx Ken x. ...
P.S. I liked dads photo but it a pity he wasn't smiling

(Keith's dad, photograph sent to him in hospital.)

This was in May, my mother had died in April on a Tuesday, the day after Easter Monday that year. My brother, when he got better, went back to his foster mother and my uncle, the one who had taken us out to the teashop, bought him another bike because his first bike was crushed. He never bought me one and he never came to see me either, but when Keith eventually recovered he decided to cycle over to Ware to see me, it was about sixteen odd miles each way. It was a Saturday morning the first time he came; it was like a miracle to me because he came unannounced and I had been feeling particularly fed up that morning and hating the chores and the loneliness. To be fair my foster mother fed him but when he came over the second time she opened the door and said, "Not you again." We were left in the garden, and he spent most of the visit repairing a puncture and never came again. Aunty didn't want to feed him and she didn't want him to come and see me, but his foster mother arranged that I should go and see him.

I went on the bus to Hertford on a Saturday and from there on another bus to St Albans and stayed one night. I had to share the boys' bedroom, Keith gave up his bed for me, I don't know where he went off to but I was in the same room as the three other evacuees who were all adolescent boys. In the pitch dark, in the middle of the night there was a thump on my bed and I thought, "Ooh, that's one of the boys". I felt gingerly down the bed and came in contact with the dog, so we shared Keith's bed together. After that I visited a couple more times, but the boys always left me alone. Although I can't recall her name any more she was in my opinion a marvellous foster mother. Keith always said she was slovenly because she didn't do any housework, preferring to run the shop she owned downstairs. I used to stay in the kitchen the whole morning when I went and help her do the week's washing up, and then she would feed me with the others and allow me to go out with my brother, and all the boys would come with us. It's strange that I can't remember this foster mother's name who was so very kind to me and always gave me a little present when I left, like a pot of Silver Shred marmalade or an apron from her shop and then she became ill and died.

I had this letter to say Keith had left there and gone to another billet because she'd died. No one realised that I'd built up a relationship with her and also my grandmother died round about that time. My foster mother had another letter from my father when I was just going out to school one morning and she said, "I've got another disappointment for you and some more bad news, your grandmother has died". I just said, "Oh really" and slammed the door and walked off and never said another word to anybody about it all because I knew it was no good, nobody would do or say anything. When my brother's foster mother died it explained why it was so difficult for her to cope with the boys, the shop and the housework because she was ill but it broke me when my grandmother died as well. It broke me because for some reason by then I was able to take in that I would never see these people again and I began to go inside myself.

Keith was put into a hostel for evacuees because there were no billets left. I went to visit him once there; he was the oldest child amongst about fifteen evacuees. I only went for the day and was with him a very short time but we had to go into the garden with all these younger children and were left responsible for amusing them, and he organised a game, Tin Can Topper it was called. We played with all these kids and then I went home, that's all I remember about the hostel, the responsibility of looking after all these children. Keith was two years older than me and after being in the sixth form for a while he left but didn't go back to Hastings, he went to London to work but I stayed in Ware. I was still very involved with school but I didn't have any social life, I felt very isolated, apart from one friend whose mother had joined her and they lived together in a flat. Sometimes they asked me round to tea but apart from that I was totally absorbed into this family, and for some reason they didn't seem to want me to have a family of my own, and in a way they were right because I had very little else in my life from that other world at all, but I still fantasised about going home one day.

On one occasion during the Blitz they took me up to the East End of London with them to see uncle's father when he was dying. I suppose they didn't know what else to do with me, but when we got there and needed to stay the night we were all shut in this room with the old man. We couldn't get out of the room because the black out wasn't strong enough, and there was an air raid going on overhead. We couldn't go to the toilet, so we had to use a bucket. There were nine people in the room all night, all members of the family except me, and the Blitz was going on outside. I thought we were going to be killed and no one would ever know what happened to me but can't remember much detail, just impressions and being led through the street in the pitch dark, like walking through black velvet.

In the council house where I was living there was a bathroom with a cold tap and a gas boiler. Aunty filled the boiler once a week and then baled the water out to fill the bath. She bathed my foster brother and then allowed me to bath in his dirty water and I got scabies. I didn't know what it was; I just knew that I was completely covered from head to foot with this intolerable itching and was tearing myself to pieces with my nails. I had bright red hair and the sort of skin that went with it, which was apparently very vulnerable and susceptible to disease. She took me to the doctor's. He said, "This child's got scabies" and she said, "She can't have that in my house, that is a dirty disease". It was living in her house I'd got it, so I had to go to hospital and was in there for two weeks. It was the old workhouse hospital and I was in a big, big general ward but in an annexe, where they put skin patients. The treatment was a hot bath every day, soaking in it as hot as you could bear and then being covered from head to foot with Sulphur ointment. I nearly died in there one day because the nurse was very busy and had to leave me in the hot bath and disappeared and I fainted because the water was too hot, but she returned before I went under the water. I vaguely remember her pulling me out over the edge of the bath and laying me down on the cold linoleum floor, that soon brought me round. When I went back to my billet I had to treat myself for a long time with ointment the doctor gave me as spots went on appearing for a long time between my fingers and toes. I always did this in secret, and never told anyone at school where I had been because I was so ashamed to have scabies.

As I developed and became a young woman something else happened but I can't remember how old I was and I never told anybody. One night, when I'd gone to bed, my foster father came into my bedroom and sat on my bed, which he had never done before and started saying things he'd never said before and kissed me. I was absolutely terrified because it wasn't an ordinary kiss, it hurt my lips against my teeth and I couldn't move to escape from it. He left but I didn't move for hours and hours. I was completely and utterly immobile; I was paralysed with fear. The next time he came back I can't remember whether he kissed me first but he started moving his hands across my body and holding my breasts in his hands. He never raped me but he just used to handle and kiss me and I couldn't tell anyone. I don't know why I couldn't tell anyone but I couldn't. I began to suffer from insomnia because he didn't come every night, and I used to lie awake and watch to see if he would come and stand silhouetted in the doorway, his arms akimbo on the doorposts before making his way to my bed. My foster mother knew that I was ill and took me to the doctors. Again I remember being in the surgery, it was a woman doctor or maybe a nurse this time and she said, "Something is worrying you?" My foster mother said, "There is absolutely nothing worrying her," and yanked me out, so that was that. I decided for myself that the only thing I could do was to hate him.

I had begun to love him because I was able to relax with him; he was fun before all this happened, the one person who could make me laugh. So I went into reverse and aunty saw, she said one day, "Look at her face, she hates you", she could interpret that, but she never asked why I suddenly started to hate him, but later on in life I realised that she may have had a pretty good idea.

Eventually my father came to see me, because I'd got to a decision stage at school, - I suppose I was sixteen by then. He decided for me that I was going to transfer to Ware Grammar School and would not go home with my own school because they were drifting back. He hadn't asked me if I wanted to, he said I was going into a pre-nursing course in the sixth form on offer at Ware Grammar School. That night he had nowhere to sleep, he'd never ever been to sleep in that house in four and a half years and the only place to sleep was in my single iron framed bed. He got into the bed and I wouldn't join him, so he said, "Come on my girl, what's the matter with you, you know I would never hurt you?" and I still wouldn't get into bed with him and he said, "That bloody B-", naming this bloke, my foster father and I thought, "He knows, he knows, he knows". Of course he didn't hurt me, I went to bed with him and went to sleep cuddled up to my dad, my own dad, who I had lost so many years ago. But the next morning after breakfast he just went back to Hastings in true 'daddy' style. He left me there to go to the sixth form and I hated it. He left me in the same house because I suppose there was nowhere else to go, was there?

I hated the sixth form at Ware Grammar School because the girls were all dressed in white blouses and skirts and I'd only got a shiny old gymslip because of course father hadn't thought about kitting me out, or what I might need. I was painfully self-conscious and was made to feel like some runt because they were so terribly cruel, the host girls, and very cocky with it. They said, "Why do you dress like a little girl"? And I remember looking at them and thinking, "I bet I know a bit more about life than you do." I hated it so much because all my own friends had gone back and after a term I decided I wasn't going to stay, I'd got to get out of there and just couldn't stand any of it at all any more. So I went to see the headmistress and I can remember standing outside her door actually shaking and saying, "I want to go back". She was wonderful; she said, "Yes, I can understand you wanting to go home". So I wrote to my father saying "I'm coming home." This was at the end of 1944, I had been away nearly four and a half years.

I don't know where the fare came from but I went up to London and Keith taught me to use the Underground and he took me to a show. It was the first show I'd ever been to, I think it was The Song of Norway but when we got to the station to go back to Ware I fainted on the station, perhaps we hadn't had anything to eat, I don't know, but I came round just in time to be thrown on the train and realised I really was becoming ill and I knew I'd got to leave. I remember leaving but not saying goodbye to anybody except my foster mother and she actually came to the station with me and then said, "I want to do my shopping," and left me standing completely alone on the platform. She went whilst I was waiting for the train.

I crossed London and when I got back to Hastings my father was there to meet me at the station, and he took me on a bus to the house. It was spotlessly clean; there was nothing in it of ours, he had got rid of every toy I'd possessed, including Knobby Sands, my teddy bear. He showed me my bed which was made and turned down ready to get in to and then he took me downstairs and said, "I'm going now, I'm going back to my base," and he just left me, and went back to sleep and live at his base for the next two nights. I'd still got my coat on and my case was just where I'd put it down; I thought, "Oh my mum must be here really", so I ran all over the house but at the same time I was thinking, "No, I know she's not here, she's dead."

I went downstairs again, but felt I couldn't stay there. In my pocket was a poem I'd written about my mum, perhaps I'd meant to show it to my dad, I read it, "How cold and still now lies my loving mother; How silent are those lips from which sweet words did flow; Our love for one another was so much it could not grow..." then I tore it up into tiny pieces and put them down the toilet. I picked up my little case, which contained all I owned in the world, and walked out the house that I'd waited four and a half years to come back to, because I just couldn't bear it. My grandfather was still living in a two-roomed flat round the corner and along the road, so I went and knocked on his door. Waiting for him to answer the door I wondered, "If he doesn't take me in, where shall I go?" But he did, he said, "Hello my girl," as though he'd left me yesterday, and took me in. He made me up a bed on his horsehair sofa in front of the warm range and I went into this deep, deep sleep of utter exhaustion and when I woke in the morning I was covered in fleabites.

Grandfather was an old man and he'd lost his daughter and his wife and let himself go, he wasn't a capable and domesticated person like my father and needed me as much as I needed him. I stayed with him and together we sorted ourselves out. I went up to the school and they wouldn't take me back because they had no pre-nursing course and the headmistress was really angry with me because I had abandoned the one she'd found for me at Ware. Anyway I needed to earn my living, so I went to work and trained as a Post Office Telephonist. I never ever went back to live in my house.

When I was seventeen my father re-married whilst I was still living with my grandfather and said that he'd found us a new mother and would I go and live with them in her house which I did, but I didn't like her. I'd lived with my grandpa for a year or so by this time, so I went to see him almost every day. Keith was still living in London when I went to live with my stepmother, he was lonely and thought it would be a good idea to come and live there with me and he came back, but he hated it even more than I did. My stepmother was very jealous of my relationship with my father, although I never knew whether I really had one. If I spoke to him she would reply, so I left home again and went to train as a nurse in London. I used to go home for a weekend to see them, but I never lived at home again. My brother left some time after I did and went to a college to train as a priest, so our hard won education paid off in the end. We both went back to our old church whilst I was living in Hastings again, it was just along the road from where we used to live. The vicarage had been bombed and the vicar's little daughter Deirdre was killed, she was two and it upset the vicar so much he moved off to a country parish. After the war a new vicar was appointed and given a new home. He set up a youth club for all the young people returning from the war, which I went to and made lots of friends, including a very special boy friend and I did find some happiness there and my faith in the church was restored. Whilst I was away I can't remember being happy, well, happy is not how I would describe it, there was always this idea that at any time I would go back. Before my mother died she used to write to me, saying "All things work together for good to those who love God" but I felt that God had deserted me, that if He was there what was this all about, this war?

It didn't feel very safe in Ware sometimes; there were bombing incidents. On one occasion they exploded a land mine, which fell nearby, but although it didn't go off it was hot and everyone was warned to take cover. I'd hardly got to the shelter and was just inside when they let it off, and the blast seemed to go in one ear and come out of the other as though there was nothing between them but sensation, and the amazing sense of a power lifting my legs as I sat down. When we got back to the house all the windows were broken, all the curtains had come down and they had been thrust under rugs by the hand of the blast. The canary Joey was dead, all his feathers had been blown off him and were scattered around the cage and the floor and he lay on his back naked with his little feet stuck up in the air. That was a terrifying experience, which I'm not going to forget. I was also alone in the deserted High Street in an air raid one day, and decided not to shelter because it was all quiet when a lone German plane came over and swooped down and I thought he was going to machine gun me, so I tried to hide in a shop doorway but it was too narrow. I looked up at him and he looked down at me through his goggles and swooped up again and away, my legs turned to jelly and I wondered why he had spared me and then had a thought that maybe he was father to a little girl at home in Germany. I had no sympathy when I got back to my billet except perhaps in the statement, "Well you daft ha'peth, you should have sheltered shouldn't you!"

I have recovered from all this because I was determined to. I felt when I met my husband I'd got to marry him. I mean I had had other boy friends; I had this one in Hastings who deserted me when I went away to train as a nurse, and one in London during my training. But when I met my husband somehow I knew that he was the one for me, and we got engaged on Easter Sunday and married in September. We had children straight away and it was a hard life but it fulfilled me in lots of ways. My husband was absolutely safe and solid and we stuck to each other. We had troubles, who doesn't? We argued at times but we were always faithful to each other. When he died I thought I was going to die too, because all this other stuff came back, this huge sense of insecurity, which I'd never lost.

The betrayal was the thing that came to me through it all, this deep sense of betrayal by my foster father, of course, and somehow by many others, including the authorities responsible for our welfare. I was left with this deep sense of betrayal, abandonment and disillusion. It's so confusing because we were all caught up and moved around in this system of evacuation; there was a need for a system, if you like, that seemed to penetrate everyone's lives, our personal lives and those of the people looking after us. It was almost as though they'd been instructed how to behave when looking after us, to keep our emotions at a distance but some were extremely kind people and did their best and most of them were basically good. Well, I want to think that people are basically good, but that seems very hard looking at some of the evidence. But I know that throughout it all somehow I've held on to the faith that my mother taught me.

Copied from Sylvia's original letters from her mother.

nice a day Sunday anyway as God is watching
over you + sees all you do, + we must
not forget Him in any way. All things
work for good, for those who love God.
                Keep smiling, my little *
+ keep happy + then I won't worry.
Write mum as soon as you can + let
me know everything, + when you write
don't forget dad as he loves you, you know
            your + grandad loved your
little note, + gran is writing to you shortly

73

# Chapter 6. 'They would be in the Crown Court today.'

## John Farmer's Story.

My name is John. I was born and bred in Hastings, at 65 Mount Pleasant Road, and I attended Mount Pleasant Junior and Infants School, as it was then. My father was a plumber and my mother, who had been orphaned at a very early age, was brought up in an orphanage until she was sixteen. I was evacuated from Hastings to Aston near Stevenage in Hertfordshire on 21$^{st}$ July 1940, which was a Sunday, from Mount Pleasant Junior School, with my younger brother who is four years younger than I am. I was just nine years of age and he was five. I remember our parents were allowed to come to the school to bid us goodbye but they weren't permitted to accompany us to the railway station, for the obvious reason that there were logistic problems with enormous numbers of people. We all had our luggage labels with our name on and, I suppose, the name of our school and a gas mask in a square cardboard box with a strap that went over our shoulder. I think we were told to take sandwiches to eat on the journey, and a drink.
I remember when we got down to Hastings station there were all these children... I'd never seen so many in one place at one time. I think we were all a bit apprehensive although we'd been prepared, I suppose, by our schoolteachers over a period of weeks before the evacuation came along, and also by our parents who told us that this was going to be a tremendously exciting adventure. We would live in the country and be very safe with cows and grass and live off the cream of the land as it were.

Well, we left Hastings by train and I remember we were forbidden to drink our drinks while we were on the train, I think people were worried about us being sick. I also remember we ate the sandwiches long before we got to London and I suppose it could have only taken a couple of hours even in those days to go to London. Then we went in buses, I think from Victoria down to Aston, there might have been a train journey involved but if there was I honestly don't remember it, I'm not clear about it. I was very young but I had the responsibility of my younger brother and remember my mother saying in particular, "You know, you're nine he's five, he's your responsibility," and I felt that very keenly. We eventually arrived in the hall of the village school which was an 'all through' school from five to fourteen. There were three classes; the school leaving age was fourteen in those days unless you attended a Grammar School.
We were taken into this village school hall, just like a lot of animals

really, because we were told to sit there and eventually people started to come in. A Mrs So and So turned up and she made it clear that she wanted only one, only a boy or only a girl, some were willing to take more than one but they wanted two girls or two boys, not a boy and a girl. Whether this was due to accommodation problems I don't know but eventually the school hall emptied except for us, we were the very last ones and I remember thinking, "Gosh, does nobody want us?" Ironically the lady who at last came to claim us lived just literally the other side of the road, she could have been there first but she turned up last. Mrs Harmer was a big lady... I can see her now - grey hair and big rosy cheeks. I don't know how old she would have been but she had a son of fourteen who was just about to leave that school, so she couldn't have been any more than in her forties perhaps; she took my brother and me.

We spent about eighteen months of our two years there. Mr Harmer, her husband, was Head Gardener of a country mansion. We lived in Aston Lodge, which was the Lodge to Aston House, owned by a man called Morton - a very elderly man he seemed to be. He must have been, I think, seventy years old. He had two unmarried daughters in their early forties and very attractive ladies they were, even I thought they were attractive and I was only nine years old; his wife had died many years previously. Mr Morton also had two cars, I think one was a Rolls Royce and the other was a Bentley and he was able to retain the services of a full time chauffeur who did other things as well. Of course petrol was rationed so there was very little petrol but practically every day he was required to clean these things and polish them; I can see this chap now washing those immaculate enormous cars. Mr Harmer the man we lived with worked for Mr Morton on a small farm with a Jersey herd, sheep and poultry. There were also big orchards and very decorative gardens and lawns and a hard tennis court.

Anyway, getting back to our billet, it was a terrible place. Mr Harmer was a very nice chap, we liked him tremendously, but he was very much dominated by his wife and he was only nice really when she wasn't there. They had a son, their only child, who left the school just as we arrived and became an assistant in an architect's office in Stevenage, which was about five miles away. He was a thoroughly objectionable character in so many ways. Mrs Harmer was constantly complaining about things we were doing. We'd come from a town and we weren't used to the uneven roads and paths of the countryside, and I must admit we seemed to be always falling over and grazing our knees and sometimes we tore our clothes by going through hedges, I suppose, but she got very, very cross. There was one occasion when we were threatened that if this sort of thing happened again we'd go to bed with no tea, and one evening it happened.

We were normally allowed to listen to the radio at six o clock, to Listen With Children with Uncle Mack, but this time we were sent to bed; we had a double bed, my brother and I. We had a drink but nothing to eat and we weren't allowed to put the light on in the bedroom and were told to stay there until eight o'clock the next morning. It was a dreadful thing to do to us. Of course there was a chamber pot under the bed, because there were no flush toilets like we'd been used to in Hastings.

We were always tearing our clothes or doing something that upset her. It got to such a point that the mother of Donald Harmer's friend Andy, who used to invite us up to tea on Sundays sometimes, got to hear what was going on. I don't know how, whether through her son or other means, but she made it clear that if ever we tore our clothes we could go to her immediately after school or during the lunch hour and she would mend them; which she did on one occasion to protect us from the emotional scars we were developing. Our foster mother used to go to Stevenage one day a week usually on a Monday and for lunch we had to come home from school. We weren't allowed into the house but had to sit under a lean-to literally, whether there was snow on the ground or ice, if it was raining or galing, and she'd leave us greasy old mutton sandwiches, no butter or marge which were rationed, and maybe jam. I've never eaten jam since and we used to take the meat out because it was so foul and just eat the bread.

We were required to go to church three times on Sundays, but before we went on a Sunday morning Mrs Harmer insisted that we wrote home to our parents each week, (which was fair enough) but she insisted that she read the letters before they were sealed. In fact she more or less dictated things to go in them, saying how happy we were and we weren't, we were very, very unhappy, but of course my mother wasn't to know that the contrary was true. My father was in the army by then, and my mother only visited us I think twice in the two years. If you were to ask, "But why didn't your mother come more often?" I don't know the answer to that question. It could be either she couldn't afford to, or it may be that she couldn't bear the emotional parting; I don't know. Every month or six weeks a coach was chartered from Hasting, we knew of course when it was coming and where it would stop, it had about three or four hours there and then it went back again. We often used to go down and see who was on it and we were disappointed except for two occasions in two years, I think we probably had prior notice that she was coming then. So I've often wondered about that and when she died in 1992 I'd never been able to ask her that question. Ultimately on one of her two visits when we went out with mum, my brother and I were able to tell her how unhappy we were because Mrs Harmer wasn't present but I don't know that she really believed us. I suppose she thought, "Well this is understandable, they're homesick," but I don't think she really appreciated how much we hated it. We had sweets sent by my parents and my aunts which were of course on ration, and they used to be put into the larder in the Harmer's house to be doled out over a period of time, which was fair enough not all to be eaten on the same day, but we know their son used to have his share and we daren't tell his mother because he could do no wrong in her eyes, absolutely no wrong at all. Oh it was a dreadful, dreadful place! But, as I say when Mrs Harmer was away for whatever reason, Mr Harmer was a charming man. It's all so silly isn't it!

The school itself, I suppose, on the whole was pretty good; well, we thought it was, even though it was only a three-class school because we were integrated with the local boys and girls. The Headmaster was a Mr Rockliff, his wife was also a teacher, he had the upper ages class 10-14, she had the middle class 7-10 and a dear lady called Miss Ockenden had what I call the Infants class, I suppose 5-7; or something like that.
It's no longer there, it's been razed to the ground and there's a housing estate on it now but I have fond memories of that school. I was very happy there, we both were. I passed my eleven plus the year after I went there when I was only nine for some experimental reason and then I did it again at ten and at eleven. The school had a garden and the boys were given a plot, while the girls did either cooking or sewing or knitting. I remember winning my first ever prize, which was for six tomato plants from the Billeting Officer Sir Malcolm someone or other for the best - kept plot with no weeds and it was absolutely immaculate. I thoroughly enjoyed Country Dancing and Natural History, which was going about learning plants, flowers, trees, shrubs and animals. So I have very happy memories of the school, but nobody ever asked us if we were happy in our billet. Nobody did, nobody ever did, either in Aston or in St Albans; nobody asked, "Are there any problems? Can we help you?" No, that was a real deficiency on the part of the authorities, I know there was a war on and they had more important things to think about, but there should have been someone there for us. Today, of course, there would be, there would be a whole army of people and if you hadn't got a problem they'd almost create one for you I think. I tried to look after my brother emotionally during that time because I did feel responsible for him and, as I say, I passed the scholarship, my eleven plus, but sadly later on he didn't.
After about eighteen months for reasons I can't quite remember we left the Harmer's house and we were taken into the big house, the Morton's house. This was going from one extreme to the other because nurse Watkins who was a Welsh lady, long since retired, had raised the two girls. She was the nanny and she was still there because she'd got a home

with them for life and she took us under her wing. There were servants of all kinds like parlour maids, gardeners, cowmen and farm workers and of course we didn't eat with the Astons, we had our own dining room. If they were at home the Morton ladies Miss E- and Miss M- would come and see us in bed at night to tuck us in but I don't think they actually kissed us. They weren't terribly maternal but they were extremely nice ladies, so we had much more going for us there than we had with their head gardener's wife.

Mr Morton himself was a dear chap, he was extremely tall, taller than I am and I'm six foot two and he had an absolutely snow-white beard; he was a director of the Army and Navy stores in London. I think he must have had other businesses as well, because he was obviously a very wealthy chap and he used to give us the opportunity of earning pocket money by weeding parts of the grounds and he would pay us so much an hour. He'd come round on a Saturday morning and I can see his hand shaking now with silver in it and he'd say, "How much do I owe you?" although he knew very well how much he owed us, and on one occasion he owed me two shillings and tuppence but he'd only got half a crown and he said, "Have you got fourpence change?" I hadn't, so he said, "Oh dear, well I'll have to pay you next week." He didn't say, "Well have half a crown" I guess that's probably how he'd made his money, I remember that so clearly.

One of the things my brother and I did when we were there was each Saturday morning we used to visit every household without exception to collect waste paper, cardboard boxes and magazines, put them into sacks and cart them down to a central collecting point; it was entirely voluntary but we enjoyed doing that. There was a man called Harry Acres who had a wooden leg as a result of injury in the First World War, he was a shoe repairer and when two of our contemporaries went to him and said, "Have you got any waste paper?" He said, "Oh no, I keep mine for John and his brother, they're the only ones who take my waste paper," so we built up quite a clientele, as it were, and were judged to be the champion waste paper collectors in the area. As a reward we were taken one Saturday afternoon in a car trailer to Bedford by a farmer to a cinema, I can't remember what film we saw, but afterwards we were given ice cream and sandwiches and things, it was a great treat. We were also encouraged to collect acorns for pig food for which we were paid a penny a pound and rose hips but I don't know how we were rewarded for those. During the autumn we were sometimes given time off school to go and pick potatoes which we thoroughly enjoyed because they allowed us to have a bonfire and bake some in their jackets in the embers for ourselves, that was great fun.

Then in '42 I went to St Albans to join the Hastings Grammar School where I had two billets, and my brother went back home. I can't remember how I transferred to St Albans but I think almost certainly we went home together; my brother stayed and I went back under the supervision of sixth formers who were always charged with escorting the first years across London and anybody else who wanted to tag along. The Grammar School had been away for two years by the time I arrived and was associated with St Albans Public School. They also used Brampton Road Secondary, Spicer Street church hall and Marlborough House, which was an old Victorian three-storied house; so we had classes in at least four different parts of the city. There was quite a bit of this going from A to B and B to C and C back to B and then D. I often turned up late because we had to walk; we weren't allowed to go by bus. M G G Hyder was the Head Master, a very eloquent and very articulate dapper little man. Either he knew what was going on in the school and did nothing about it or he didn't know but either way I condemn him totally. He wouldn't survive as a headmaster today because of the treatment meted out by his staff. It was absolutely appalling, they would be in the Crown Court today; well 60% would be in the Crown Court, they really would.

Bill Barnet the art master who had a son in the form above me, had the most vicious temper, he would physically assault people. Pearce the Latin master would do likewise, Rushby-Smith the geography master likewise. They'd sort of hit you round the head, get you up and throw you from one side of the room to the other. It never happened to me but I was petrified, I couldn't learn when I didn't know whether I was going to be the next one to be asked a question and if I didn't know the answer or I gave the wrong answer then I was at the mercy of these psychological thugs, miscreants I call them. Then you had the other extreme like Connersby who was known as Ding. He was the English master who was a very nice man but he wasn't cut out to be a schoolmaster, he was constantly 'ribbed' from the time he went in to the class until he went out, he couldn't control a class of two let alone one of thirty; how he survived that poor man without going mental I've no idea. He'd write something on the board and he'd believe he'd heard somebody shout out something and sometimes they had and sometimes nobody had said anything and he'd turn round and say, "Come out the boy who said that." He tried to be ever so fierce and of course he just couldn't be fierce, it was terribly sad. It was a case of absolute extremes and it was dreadful. There was a parson Taylor who was a vicious thug too and Fergusson who taught geography, he was the headmaster's secretary as well and another very unpleasant character.

I had two billets whilst I was in St Albans. The first billet was with a lovely lady and her husband, who was very nice too. They had two sons and a daughter and when she found she was expecting a fourth child that was the reason for us having to move. The two boys went to an ordinary secondary school so of course they had no homework in the evening and there were no facilities for doing ours; also they had the radio on and the boys would say, "Come on, let's go and play football", so that didn't help matters. The man who was our foster father worked in some sort of factory during the day but at night he was a poacher. On Saturday nights he would take the four of us out with him, his two sons who were twelve and thirteen at the time, Bobby (another boy from Hastings) and me; I was eleven. He was a dead shot with a catapult an absolutely dead shot, I've never seen anybody so accurate, he used to spend hours searching for the right size and shape of pebble, which was critically important. We used to go out on a moonlit night and see the pheasants and partridges roosting and his success rate with the birds in flight was a canny seven out of ten, they would just fall down. He'd pick them up and put them in his poacher's great big coat and then I'm sorry to say he used to encourage us to steal from people's allotments, cabbages, sprouts, carrots... we fed well. Then we'd go to the odd orchard at midnight and to do this we'd need to cross the London to St Albans railway line because they were on the other side. We fed extremely well in that house; pheasant was very commonplace at weekends.

I kept in touch with this foster mother who moved from St Albans to Harpenden, and one time when I called on her she didn't know I was coming. Although her husband had separated from her by then, she had literally just come back from his funeral, it was a most embarrassing time to call, but she was so pleased to see me. She was reminiscing back to the times when he took us poaching and she said, "Yes, we lived all right, but he was a very mean man." When he brought in a pheasant or a hare or a rabbit or vegetables, he used to assess the value of those things and then deduct it from the money he would otherwise have given her.

It was when this lady was expecting her fourth child that we had to move and we went into another part of the city. At this second billet we were often late for school because we were forbidden to get up before 8 o 'clock or something. We were billeted with a brother and a sister where the brother worked in London as a solicitor's clerk and used to catch the train from St Albans to London each day and his sister looked after him, she was unmarried. By the time we got down to the bus stop, the buses which were relatively few and far between were often full by the time they reached our stop, and we had to wait for the next one, which made us late and several times we were caned by Baker, who used to cane anybody for anything. There was nobody to appeal to; if you said, "Look this was it," it was never believed at all; it was dreadful. I couldn't do any homework either because there were no facilities in either billet so it's not surprising that I did extremely badly in my academic work.

Even on a Sunday we had to stay in bed until something like ten or ten-thirty, because this chap who had worked so hard during the week as a solicitor's clerk had to have a lie in. I think we had a slight snack at eleven o'clock or something and were then sent out with, "Don't come back 'till three o'clock", when we'd have lunch literally at three o'clock in the afternoon. We used to go and join some of our friends and when they were going back for tea we'd be going back for lunch. I suppose they wanted a bit of time to themselves. They weren't unkind to us; they were just strange. They were very set in their ways and not married, or used to children and I suppose they probably had no choice about taking us because there was a certain element of compulsion about taking an evacuee if you'd got a spare bed. Neither of us was happy there, but Bobby stayed on and eventually came back with the school in '45 or '44; he became a road research scientist and has long since retired because he was still unhappy.

I came back to Hastings for a holiday in the summer of 1943, and begged my mother not to send me back. My father was in the army so he had no involvement in that decision and it took a long time to persuade her, I think she was very proud of the fact that I'd passed for the grammar school as most people were in those days and she thought it was going to lead perhaps to a better career than my father had been able to obtain. He was one of ten, so he didn't have much chance. Well, eventually I persuaded her and I think she probably realised it was the right thing to do, that I'd be much happier at what was initially called Hastings Emergency Boys or something and then it became Hastings Secondary Modern School for Boys up in Priory Road, it's still there of course. And there I went from being at the bottom to the top in every subject except art, music and PE. Going back to Hastings was like going from one extreme to the other, I was very happy indeed. My mother was wonderful although she wondered for some time whether she'd done the right thing by allowing me to come home and leave the Grammar School and she was probably worried about what my father would think. In the end I never did know what he thought; he never voiced his opinions one way or the other to me and for some reason I was never very interested in my father, I'm not quite sure why. Probably my mother had briefed him about school and was able to convince him that I was not doing badly because of my exam results and the reports that I used to take home.

Hugh Read was a totally different kind of headmaster, very firm and very fair, a great big tall man; he was chairman of the Juvenile Bench at the time. He got a DSO, (a medal for distinguished service), in the First World War, which always impressed me although he never spoke about it. He taught me to play chess in an out-of-school chess club and it was he who persuaded me to go into Local Government as a career. I wanted to learn farming but my parents didn't want me to go into farming and Hugh Read was absolutely horrified. Unknown to me there must have been some collusion between them because he called me into his office one day and said there was a wonderful opportunity going in the Education Department in Hastings, "For somebody just like you". He pointed out and my parents agreed, that it was a good job with security. I would have been fifteen in February, this was December 1945 and I was persuaded to go at least for the interview. I went to see Norman King who was then the director of Education to be interviewed not really knowing what I was about because I really wanted farming. He asked me a number of questions and for some reason I didn't call him sir through ignorance I suppose, although I'd always called my schoolmasters 'sir'. He said to me, "Do you ever call anybody sir?" When I responded that I didn't realise it was required or appropriate I got the job. So I left school illegally of course with the collusion of the Director of Education. Of course in the Education Department at Hastings I was called a junior clerk but I was the office boy. It was at the time when service men were being de-mobbed and they were setting up teacher training colleges, there was one in Eastbourne, which we had some involvement with in Hastings. Hastings on the Hudson in New York was twinned with our Hastings. They very proudly sent us lots of things during the war and even in 1946 after the war had ended they sent shoes across, enormous numbers of shoes. Plimsolls we called them then, trainers now I suppose and other shoes and I had the job of allocating these to thirty-three schools in Hastings from a warehouse somewhere. I had a taxi provided as I went round to all these schools; I don't know how long it took me to deliver them.

There used to be a Hastings Commercial Evening Institute in Portland Place, just opposite where Marks and Spencer's is now. A man called Hardwick was the principal. To cut a long story short I assisted him as a registrar, that was my title, taking the money for people enrolled on evening classes and checking the registers, and policing the caretaker, and making arrangements for examinations to be supervised and so on, which was very lucrative. I did a short-hand and typewriting course but I never did master the short-hand because there were too many female distractions in the class but the typewriting I mastered and it has stood me in good stead for the last forty or fifty years. I was looking at the receipt the other day, which I had made out to myself. A two-term course in shorthand and typewriting was sixpence in old money. I was glad I changed to agriculture and so were my parents although I quite enjoyed education and made some very good friends who I still have.

The war must have been affecting my emotional world a lot, it ruined my education really, because I eventually left school with no academic qualifications whatever. I sought to rectify that later by going to Evening Classes and doing Pre-Matric and Matriculation studies but it was no thanks whatever to the Hastings Grammar School that I made progress. I would have coped better if I hadn't been evacuated and attended the Grammar School in Hastings. The fact is there was no support, there was no one to talk to about the billets, people just thought you hadn't done your homework so you must be punished. They didn't ascertain, "Why hasn't this person done his homework?" They just didn't want an explanation; the only place we could have done our homework was in the bedroom, which we both shared. We had separate twin beds but there was no heating, there was no central heating in many houses in those days and people certainly didn't want to put on an electric fire, or put an extra light on or something. That was the terrible deficiency; there was no welfare officer to talk to or anyone else; we can't have been alone in our experience; there must have been lots of similar instances and I know I would have done better if I'd had my mum to go home to, instead of having four billets in three years.

My father survived the war. His father died in the First World War and my mother's father, she was orphaned really early. It wasn't talked about so I don't know what effect it had on the family. My own experience of the blitz was in the first place, believe it or not, when a land mine dropped right in the middle of a river about a quarter of a mile from where we were living. It created a big crater, which we were forbidden to swim in but we did. Yes, and then in 1941 my brother and I were woken up and the whole village was woken by the most enormous series of very loud explosions and the whole sky was a fire of flame at Aston from a very hush, hush place, and later we found out that it was an enormous ammunition depot that went up. Whether it was sabotage or some dreadful accident we never did learn but I thought the end of the world had come. It was the other side of a large field. It couldn't have been more than five or six hundred yards away, and that was very frightening for everybody because nobody knew what had happened. We were still living in the lodge with the Harmers. It wasn't a factory; it was just a store about which there was always a certain amount of mystery and high security and all sorts of rumours about what went on there but everybody knew after the whole lot went up. I don't recall any bombs dropped in St Albans whilst we were there, I know it wasn't badly affected.

The only thing I remember with horror was the doodlebug. I was doing a paper round in Hastings one Saturday morning when the very first one came over and it was just above tree top height. It kept going. I saw this thing and I was absolutely petrified, I remember spread-eagling myself against the wall of a house; there was nobody else about. They probably thought it was a motorcycle going along or something, fortunately it went on and I remember going back to the paper shop with my undelivered papers feeling terrible. After that first one, when we were in school we used to have doodlebug duties in pairs. We were up on the roof looking towards the sea with glasses and as soon as we saw them coming we blew whistles and everyone in the school got down under their desks.

My mother had been brought up in a Church of England orphanage so she used to go to church but she didn't take us. She went to high church to confession and I remember my father saying to her one day, "Why do you have to go to church to confess, you look after us very well. You cook for us, you clean for us?" After that she never went to church again; he wasn't religious at all, quite the contrary, but they sent us to Sunday school in Hastings and in St Albans we went to a Sunday morning service and Sunday afternoon children's service, which was compulsory and then I went to evening service and sang in the choir. In fact we used to take it in turns to pump the organ. There used to be a ritual in Aston after the evening service in the summer months when it was light, the whole congregation would leave church and I should think that 90% of it stayed together and everyone went right round the perimeter of the village. As most people got to their houses they dropped off. Everybody, men, women and children would all go on this walk and it was rather pleasant in a way. As you went along the way you caught up with the local gossip, so and so is doing so and so, a new crop is planted or a tree had been felled or somebody had died.

My experiences during the war must have formed the foundation of my philosophy of trying to be understanding and consider other people's points of view. It did have quite a profound effect, I'm always listening to what other people think, not necessarily agreeing with them but at least hearing them out. As a college principal of course that is a pretty important part of managing a large college and making decisions and I like to give people what I didn't have.

This takes me back to the Grammar School, to Pearce who was a Latin master, he was one of the most savage apart from Bill Barnet, I think I'd put him the worst. My mother used to send me the Hastings Observer every week and one day I happened to have it on my desk and he came along and saw it and said, "Oh, do you mind if I borrow that?" "No, that's all right". And thereafter at this particular lesson each week he used to come up and ask if he could borrow it. Well, that was an insurance policy frankly against getting beaten up by this thug, absolutely true, I didn't get beaten up like so many people did. Oh no, I wasn't beaten up by anybody but the fear was always there. If you couldn't conjugate verbs or something you were either thick or stupid or not trying or not listening.

I don't recall us ever being punished at home. My mother certainly never smacked us, but I remember my father would occasionally cuff us round the ear until my mother strongly objected, saying he could damage our hearing and then it didn't happen again. No, my parents were able to do it by using example or words, we were never smacked, but we were shouted at and threatened from time to time.

I stayed in the Education Department until I was eighteen and was then called up. I did two years in the RAF and decided I was old enough to make my own mistakes and still wanted to go into farming. I then went to see a man called Jessei who was principal of what was then the East Sussex School of Agriculture in Lewes and tried to persuade him to take me on a course in agriculture. One of the requirements was a year's practical experience, so when I was de-mobbed on the 29th June 1951 he said, "Well you had better come and work on the college farm, for July and August, so you have eight or ten weeks before the course starts." I was very grateful and again casting modesty to one side, at the end of that year the farm foreman one day said to me, "Unofficially and off the record mate, you're the top student, mate, don't tell anybody mate." Then the following day, covered in embarrassment he came back and he said, "Mate, you're a bloody fool". "I beg your pardon!" "Why didn't you do a grass collection?" You were required to do a grass collection, which I couldn't get interested in and didn't do it and this had come to light in the final staff meeting. So instead of being the top student, I was the 'runner up' to the top student but for someone who came from a non-farming background I was quite pleased with that.

I went to Plumpton for three years and based my whole career on pig production, believe it or not, after giving a talk about pigs without any preparation. I went to the National College in Shropshire for two years. Then I got a job as an assistant farm manager on a big estate in Sussex in Pulborough, then I came to Bicton for ten years and then back to Shropshire as Vice Principal for five years and I was a Principal for the last fourteen. Sadly, my father didn't live to see me make it - he died when I was a student. I've got two sons, one is a civil engineer and the other one's a hotel and catering graduate. I wouldn't have sent them to boarding school even if I could have afforded to. I can't understand why you would have children and then send them away for their most formative years. Evacuation, no it certainly wasn't a very happy time for me.

**This is the group of children evacuated to Aston from Mt. Pleasant School.** (John is standing behind Peggy and her brother and his brother is peeping through).

**Peggy and her brother**

# Chapter 7. 'It won't take long, you'll be home by Christmas.'

## Peggy Howe's Story.

My name is now Peggy Howe but when the war started it was Peggy Brasier. I lived in the Old Town of Hastings in a very, very prominent position where you could see all the valley, the fishing boats coming into the harbour and the wonderful picture of the seagulls flying down and picking up what they could as the boats came in. As we were so close to the sea my dad took me down to the beach sometimes at about half past six in the morning in the summer for a swim, then I would dash home in my raincoat and get ready to go off to school, it was great fun. Opposite our house was a big bank and my dad helped us to make a tree house with a couple of planks of wood. In the summer my brother and I would have picnics up there in our own private tree house, it was one of our favourite pastimes.

My father was the maintenance manager at a big Hollingsworth garage where the local doctor had his car serviced every Friday, and dad would collect us from school in it when he returned it to the doctor. It was a great treat to have a ride in this beautiful car because we didn't have a car of our own. In fact we led a very simple sort of life, there was nothing very exciting about it, because nobody was terribly rich in those days and we were just ordinary people, but a very close knit family. My brother is a year younger than me so I was his carer at all times, even when playing in the tree house, but we had a lot of fun together. On Saturdays we went to the town and were treated to a Rupert book, which was a great treasure, and then on Sundays we were sent to one Sunday School in the morning and another for younger children in the afternoons at the same church - Emmanuel up on the hill. My father taught us three rules: to always say our prayers, and clean our teeth, and the third was to make sure we had clean shoes. It's a funny thing but my brother and I have always remembered to keep these rules, keeping ourselves clean inside and out which I suppose is quite important, and I still go to Emmanuel church now, fifty odd years later. It has played a very important part in my life.

My mother couldn't work, she was always at home because she had very poor health, she had about eight operations and was always sickly and partially blind. My dad took care of her and we did things for her as well. Although I was very young to do it, one of my jobs was to clean the grate because the dust got in her eyes, and I often used to sweep the floor and make the bed, all the dust-making jobs. My mum was a very quiet lady, with what I realised later in life was an inferiority complex, which is sad because she was a very loving lady and always there for us, I can't remember her ever shouting at us or smacking us or anything like that.

My father was much firmer, but I can't say he meted out much punishment, and when he did he couldn't carry out his threats. On one occasion when I was told that I couldn't visit my aunt Vera on a Sunday afternoon because I'd been naughty I was sent to bed, it was a treat we always looked forward to. Off went my mum and brother and dad stayed at home with me but after a while he relented and let me get up and go with him, and to boot he bought me some sweets in the High Street on the way, so he was quick to forgive. Of course we weren't perfect children, but life was mainly very, very quiet but it was a good childhood in a loving family.

When the threat of war came people were talking about it, but I never really took it seriously, I suppose, until my dad joined the Special Constabulary. He was number thirteen. We weren't superstitious but I do recall that number, and I thought it was strange when he went out in the evening in uniform to train, looking very, very important, and he was issued with a gas mask.

At that time, 1939, I was about ten and a half and I remember I was sitting on the floor in our front room leaning against my dad's legs as he sat in his armchair and he held my hand as Chamberlain said on the wireless, "We are now at war with Germany." My mum cried and said, "What about the children?" Her question was answered when some time later we heard we were going to be evacuated and they both agreed we should go away with the others but dad reassured us by saying, "Don't worry, it won't take long, you'll be home by Christmas," and of course I believed him.

The news came through first at my school, Mount Pleasant Junior.

Our teachers were Miss Prue, Mr Broadbent and Mr Carpenter who taught maths. We wore blue, yellow and green bands for PE teams and at assembly the headmaster Mr Hopkins would conduct, and his face used to go red as he willed us to sing Jerusalem. He was a lovely, lovely man but very strict, there was no messing about in Mr Hopkin's school or it was the cane, but it didn't matter in those days because that was the way they did it, and if your parents were told, they would react by saying that you must have deserved it. Discipline was to the fore and I think it did us good and gave us boundaries. We wouldn't step over the line and the teachers were always 'Sir' or 'Miss,' because we were taught to respect our elders.

On the day of evacuation we were taken from Mount Pleasant School on buses to Hastings station. Our parents weren't allowed on to the station, but many of them stood on a bridge over the railway. We all had gas masks, labels, two sandwiches, an orange and a bar of chocolate, it was almost like a picnic. On the train we were told to stay close to our brothers and sisters. It was all very exciting, like going on an outing. They said we were going to live with other people for a while, because the coast was dangerous and it was going to be safer for us. I knew what they meant because a few days before we left my stepbrother had come to stay for a while and had taken us to Marks & Spencer's to buy us a little case each in which to pack all our belongings. As we came along the sea front on the way back home we saw a convoy going down the Channel, and lots of people stood and watched as a German plane came over, and we saw it come down in flames into the sea and one of the ships was on fire. I was so frightened I ran all the way home, and it seemed much more frightening to stay in Hastings, so going away was made to feel like a picnic, that is, until we arrived and were shepherded out of the train and taken to a big house. There we were divided up into sections of about forty children at a time and put in a coach to go on another journey, it was all our class that was sent together. We made our way to Aston, which is just outside Stevenage, and were taken to the main school hall. Some kind ladies gave us some more sandwiches and a glass of orange, but there were a lot of people standing around looking at us, and I found it quite horrible. I didn't like them because I knew who they were and soon they were going to point a finger and say, "I'll have him or her". I was frightened because we were like animals, being chosen - "Which one do you want?" My brother started to cry and I said to him, "You stay with me, we won't part, we'll stay together."

All the children seemed to be going, until towards the end there were two other boys with the same surname as us. They thought we were all related and must be brothers and sister, and nobody wanted four. We knew them from school, but we weren't related. Somebody didn't mind having two boys, but nobody wanted a boy and a girl, so we were the odd two out, literally the last ones to go, it was horrible, horrible. We were taken in this huge great car by a kind lady who said, "You had better come and live with me for a while", and we believed she was kind and was going to look after us. In her huge gentry house we were given a bedroom each but we felt too far apart and my brother came and slept with me because he was still crying and very frightened. When we got up the next morning the lady said, "Well you can't stay here because you are too far from the village." She didn't really want any evacuees, but had just taken us there because they didn't know what else to do with us. We were ushered back to the school hall again. The village policeman came in and said he would have one child and a very, very posh lady came and said she would have a child as well. The other two boys had been put with her head gardener, so she took my brother, so that the boys could all be together on her estate. The policeman took me, so we were separated. It was sad, but we used to sit near each other in school every day and would play together in the afternoons but he never settled, he was never really happy. He was billeted with the cook at the big house. She always forgot to light the boiler and would send my brother out to chop wood and it got to more wood and more wood. She was trying to keep herself out of trouble, because if there was no hot water for madam to bath the cook got into trouble. She leaned on my brother, a little nine year old chopping wood and he had to clean out the rabbits, he was very, very unhappy.

I was worried about my brother and wanted him near me and thought, "Why should they treat my brother like that? Why should they make him unhappy?" Every time I saw him he was crying over something, I hated that and I wanted to go and say, "You mustn't be unkind to my brother." I was all right. The policeman and his wife were beautiful people, I used to call them auntie and uncle. Sometimes they used to let my brother come and play with me and have tea and I think they did a bit of scouting around to say that he was not being treated properly, but there again the lady of the house who had taken him in knew nothing of this because he had been placed in the hands of the staff. He was in the charge of the cook, parlour maid and housekeeper of the big house, he was in their charge. He had all his food in the servants' hall, so the people who owned the house, the gentry, didn't know what was going on because they didn't mix with evacuees, they wouldn't.

School was a bit difficult because the evacuees were sort of segregated at the beginning. It took about a year to get used to each other and start to play together, and I put it down to one of the teachers whose name was Mrs Rockliff, a little short, fat lady who was very, very strict. For her it was a case of, "We're all here together, we are all going to learn and they've as much right to learn as we have, so let's get on with it". She bound us together. A Miss Ockenden had the younger children and my brother went into her class. You can imagine the chaos because it was from five to eleven years old with two teachers, so I don't know how we ever managed to learn anything with forty or fifty in each class, the evacuees all mixed in with the village children. After a while we were that mixed that we became friends in the end, there's no other way of living your life. Once we got over that border we were all right, and because we were sitting next to them in class, although it took a long time, we would begin to play together in the playground and it sorted itself out; but some of the children were very, very homesick. I was all right and, looking back, I feel I can say to be truthful that I did enjoy my time when I was evacuated. But there were times when I was very sad, they were when I saw my brother crying and when I came home from school at dinnertime and found a letter from my mum. If there was a letter, the lady where I lived would put it in the dining room window so I could see it as I came in. It was so thoughtful of her, but it always made me cry. When I read the letters the only thing I wanted to see was, "We are coming to see you" or "We are coming to bring you home". They did come and see us about once a month at first in a car from Hollingsworth where my dad worked. For a while they would bring food and my foster parents let them have meals with us, but because of the rationing they found a caravan in a field where they could stay for the week-end and we would go to them in the caravan for tea. They arrived on Friday and went home on Sunday but they never went to where my brother was staying, and my mum was petrified of a horse that lived in the field. It was sad to say goodbye when they went back to Hastings, but we could always look forward to the next time: but later there was no next time, because my dad had a stroke and could no longer drive a car, so the visits came to an end. This was about two years into the war and came at a time when although we had been evacuated to a safe place we could see London burning during the blitz. It now seems strange to recall the reflection of those fires, "Oh they're blitzing London."

Much later on the other things that were so scary were the doodlebugs, we would hear them coming and then the engine cut out and at that point they would crash land on anything. There were no pilots in them, it was very, very frightening. We had a couple of landmines in the village too, although on the outskirts of the village, which again was quite frightening. I say it was frightening but a group of us from school found a big bomb crater in a wood full of water and coming from the seaside we had nowhere to swim for a long time and we thought that it would be a bit of fun to use this bomb crater for swimming. We didn't make too much a habit of it because we had to go in there with no clothes on, we daren't go back to our billets with all our clothes wet, or we would have had to say what we were doing, so that was a bit of a risky thing to do with friends but thinking about all those daring things is the lighter side. Harvest time was always great fun as well. We were encouraged to go into the fields after school, potato picking and putting sheaves of wheat into shocks or shocks into sheaves, whichever way round it was, and I always used to like to glean round the edge of the field, pick up a big handful of wheat and then wind another piece round it. You were allowed to keep what you gleaned and I would take these home to the village policeman and his wife, and they would hang them in their shed and feed their chickens on these gleanings, so that was very helpful.

The one thing I did find a bit scary was when the tractor got near the middle of the field. Everyone was allowed to stand on the edge of the field and the rabbits were shot as they came out. The rabbits were closed in, forced into the middle of the field and in the end push they all came out and were shot. But they were all shared. If you'd got six men with guns and twelve or fourteen rabbits, they would share the rabbits out with whoever was there. That was good, but there were no refrigerators in those days, so we all had rabbit stew for about a week.

On Sundays we used to go for long walks right round the village after church. It was a lovely road, right round what we called the back road round Aston. My foster parents had one little boy called John, who was about four years younger than me, and he used to come along with us; he was a lovely little boy. Then just before I left, the lady had another baby, that she called Zelda and she asked my parents to be Godparents to their daughter. That made us into a really close-knit family, which was nice. Somebody brought my parents up when Zelda was baptised in the local church called St. Mary's, and then my brother and I were confirmed.

By this time I was twelve and we had both passed the scholarship. I took mine and my brother took his the following year but my parents didn't let us move because we were settled in the village where we were living. Well, George, my brother, was happier by now and he didn't want to go if I didn't go. My father wouldn't let me go, so it meant of course that we both stayed. I was upset at first because some of the other parents had let their children go and I was sad that they went and I couldn't. I was worried, I wanted to go on to further education because what was I going to do if I left school at fourteen? But I couldn't express this worry because I wasn't in a position where I could say to my parents, "I want to go and I'm going." If they said we were not going, that was that.

I think I do realise too the relationship that I had with the people that I was living with was very special, they were very, very, kind to me. He was a very special man, the policeman, because at night he would go out in his uniform and he would take his gun, his rifle or whatever it was and strap it on the cross bar of his bike. I used to say to him, "Why are you taking a gun?" And he'd say, "I'm going to guard the king and the queen." And when I laughed he'd say, "You don't believe me, do you?" And I said, "No, why are you taking the gun, where are they, where are the king and queen?" Then later I found out that there was a big tunnel in Hertfordshire, and the king and queen used to come out on a train and go into this tunnel. The villages all around would send two policemen each night to guard the two entrances to that tunnel and I thought that was very privileged. When uncle John went out on his bike with his gun, he just used to wink at me and say, "King and queen". I thought he was wonderful.

We came home a couple of times, the first time we came back to Hastings it was all quite quiet. The following year we came home again, but by that time the bombing was getting worse. There was an entrance to the caves which are down underneath the West Hill at Hastings, and on one particular occasion the sirens went and before we had a chance to realise where we were going my mother said, "Come on we've got to go into the caves and you've got to run all the way." The German planes were going up through the valley of the Old Town, just machine gunning, and I remember the bullets coming down in Croft Road and hitting the milk bottles and it's a sound I just cannot bear any more, the sound of smashing glass. The milk bottles just splintered and there was glass going all over the place as we were running to the caves. On another occasion during that two weeks holiday we were sitting in our front room after the sirens had gone and this Messerschmitt came up through the valley of the Old Town. We could see the pilot, which just shows how low the plane was, and he was just sitting there machine gunning everywhere. That was the last time we ever came home; if I remember rightly our parents sent us back the day after because it was so frightening... it was unbelievable. We wanted to go, we wanted to go away again because at night-time we used to sleep in the caves, which was fine because we knew we were safe down there, but we didn't like it when we came out of the caves to live in the town. We could never go anywhere when we came home, so we were either in the house in Croft Road or in the caves. I can't remember going shopping with my mum or anything like that, so it was really pointless coming home... and to think that it was summer time and where we'd been evacuated to they were having a wonderful time because they were helping with the harvest, but at night time even there we didn't feel safe because of the bombing of London.

It must have been fairly early on when we went home. Hastings was in a 'no go' area, you had to have a pass to get in and out of the town, so it must have been in 1941 or '42, when the bombing was getting bad. My father had a stroke very early on after he was machine-gunned going across the West Hill one day. He worked at Hollingsworth and he used to walk across the West Hill and then down what they called The Steeps into the Old Town. He was machine-gunned coming across there one day, so he just lay down and feigned dead and when the plane had gone and there was no fear of it coming back he got up and ran. He wasn't injured at all but I think that must have contributed to him having a stroke.

In the village there were two landmines, one didn't go off and we all had to be evacuated from our foster homes 'till they got rid of that one; but it was the doodlebugs that were the worst ones. You looked out the window and saw them go by with this great big flame coming out the back and then they stopped. Two or three times I said to my brother, "Get under your bed when you see them". As the war went on and we got round to invading France things became easier in Hastings and people could come back because the fear of invasion was gone.

My brother came home first because he wanted to be an apprentice coachbuilder at Hollingsworth and my father who was by then able to come up and see me said, "You've got two choices, you either come home and we find you a job, or you stay here and do a job that is going to be sensible for the rest of your life". I said I wanted to go into a factory, because the factories were still dishing out batteries and bullets and bombs in Stevenage at a big munitions factory there. I said, "I want to go there because that is where all the girls are going" and he said, "No, if you're going anywhere, there's nothing else for you to do but to go into domestic service". "Well I don't really want to do that, dad." "Well I'm sorry, that is your choice. If you go into domestic service, you are going to learn something and be with people that will stand you good for the rest of your life, so what do you want to do?"

I can see and hear him saying it now, "What are you going to do?" Then "That is the best thing for you. You'll learn how to cook and clean; you'll learn how to run a house. You're a girl and that is going to be the most important part of your life." "All right then, I will go into domestic service, where shall I go and work?" "I've got you a job," he said. He had already got me a job before he came to see me in the house that my brother was in for four years in Aston Dean, and I went obediently. My brother came home to go and work in Hollingsworth and I stayed there and went into domestic service in exactly the same house.

That horrible lady (the cook) had gone and I started there as under-house-maid, for about eight months. I had to have the front door step scrubbed by six-o-clock and the brass cleaned because it was not to be seen that a member of staff should walk through the main hall when madam was about. I had to do my job and be out of the way. Then I was promoted to housemaid. We all used to wear uniform and mine was a green dress with a white cross-over apron and a white cap and then I was parlour maid for a little while, replacing one who had left, she was such a miserable person I was glad she left and I took her place. I wore my green uniform in the morning and in the afternoons and for serving at table I used to have to wear royal blue and white. I had to have a clean apron, collar, cuffs and a clean cap every day.

Well, after I'd been there about a year my father bought me a signet ring for my birthday. I served the lady and her sister with their soup and one thing and another and as I took the empty plates out to the waiter trolley outside the dining room Miss E- came out to me. She said, "I'm very sorry but I don't remember giving you permission to wear a ring." I said "My father gave it to me for my birthday." "Well, I'm sorry it is not allowed, you do not wear a ring, you do not wear a necklace and you wear no lipstick." I was horrified, and thought, "Well, I've got right through the evacuation without doing anything terribly wrong and now I'm in dreadful trouble" because I wore a signet ring. I was just turned fourteen and I suppose she thought at fourteen and wearing a ring, if I chanced putting lipstick on I might finish up as a wayward girl. I mean who knows, to do a dreadful thing like that! Anyway I still stuck it and I was quite happy until I was about seventeen when the lady of the house moved. She'd bought another house in Buckinghamshire and took all her staff with her. I was very, very upset to leave Aston because of my friends but she said to me, "When I go back to Aston for a day I will take you with me." Something happened the first time she went so that she couldn't take me and I was absolutely devastated. Miss E- just went off in her car, back to Aston for the day and I was left behind. She said she couldn't take me because there wasn't room in the car.

So then I did the most daring thing of my life. I packed up the possessions that I had in a case and a hatbox that she had given me and I left. I just walked out and caught the train to Paddington and managed to get myself across London to Victoria station and I trained home to Hastings. My parents were out. I had to sit on the doorstep and wait for them to come home, with my hatbox and my suitcase. I was seventeen and my mother was horrified. She just couldn't work out what I had done. I'd been away seven years. When they came in they made me go straight to the telephone box to tell Miss E- that I was home and my father said, "Did you write a letter of apology?" I said, "Well I'm not going back because she let me down," and I would not go back but I've been back since, about twelve years ago just to have a look round the place.
My parents were very, very cross when I came back. I was upset because my mother took me straight into my bedroom and the first thing she said to me was, "Are you all right?" And I said, "Of course I'm all right". "Well, I mean are you going to have a baby?" And I said, "No, why?" "Well, why have you come home?" And I said, "I've come home because Miss E- let me down and I'm unhappy, I wanted to come home and I am not going to have a baby." I was so upset to think that my mother thought that of me. She thought that was the only reason I had come home and I was so upset, so upset and it took a long time for me to settle back down into living at home. One day I said to my mum, "Shall I

clean the knives and forks?" and she said "Why?" "Well, when I was in service I always used to clean the knives and forks." And she said, "But they were silver and these are not." And she said, "You are home now and you will accept home for what it is." And I thought, "Oh dear, that's another knock down". My mother thought I might have got sort of - above my station because it brought out her inferiority complex and it brought out a lot for me after I got home because I thought, "Why does she feel like that, we're as good as anybody else sort of thing?" but she just couldn't cope with it.

For me, I suppose living with gentry... and they were definitely pure gentry, was a wonderful experience. I mean I loved to see people in evening dress, dressed for dinner and I didn't understand all that when I was young. Charlie Bassett, one of the sweet people, came and a Commander on a submarine would come to dinner - all those sort of people. Although I wasn't one of them I learned to mix with them and really they were very, very nice people. I've got a real coral necklace that was given to me by one of the sisters, I've had it valued for about a hundred pounds when I had a new gold clasp put on it,. There were the two sisters, Miss E- and Miss M- where I worked, and Miss M- gave me this coral necklace while I was there; it's the treasure of my life and I thought it was lovely of them to give me something like that and Miss E- gave me a watch, but that didn't last as long as the necklace.

My father's decision about what he wanted for me was right, so right. He was a more gentle person; much more gentle and glad to have me back because my dad and I were one and my mum and my brother were the other one. I fitted in all right with my brother but not brilliantly, not like when we were evacuated because I felt I was the carer for him when I was away. But when I came home he'd been home about eighteen months and I was the intruder then. Yes, when I stayed away he was the one; he was the kingpin in the house. When I came home we had to go back to sharing again and it was very difficult. I'd started to build my own life with my brother not there, because I no longer had responsibility for him, I only had to look after myself and then, as I say, he became kingpin at home. I was pleased to be relieved of that responsibility because I was broken hearted to see him cry, there was nothing I could do, only cuddle him and a cuddle from your sister is nothing like a cuddle from your mum. We did go through that period when we both came home from the war and it was difficult but I love him dearly now.

He's not only my brother that I love but he's my best friend, although he lives in Hampshire he really is my best friend. We both got married. I got married first and he was Crucifer at my wedding and then he got married, I didn't take part in his wedding but I went to it. He's got two children and I had two, we're Godparents to each other's to keep the family unit close knit. I settled down in Hastings after the war, I didn't want to go anywhere else, I stayed here then but really the experiences I had with the gentry were good because they really were real gentry.

When I look back on my evacuation I must say I think I enjoyed the experience, anyway I enjoyed the nice things that happened when people changed and got to love us like the children who accepted us in the end at school and became friends and made me happy. But the fear of the war itself was horrifying to me. We had a lovely organist at St Mary's church, where my brother and I were in the choir. He was shot down in his plane and he lost both his legs. He came to church after he got over the shock of it all but he couldn't play the organ because he couldn't use the pedals, he was such a young man and he was so lovely; but as I say the horror of war will always be with me. You can't say that it doesn't have any affect on you. I cannot and I will not watch a war picture because I cannot see anything entertaining in it at all. OK you might follow the leading star through and then he gets shell-shocked and everything else, and then he comes home and they all live happily ever after. I know what it was like in the war but I don't think it's the thing we need to look at for entertainment. To me it doesn't entertain; it makes me feel even now frightened. I still to this day cannot bear the sound of an air raid siren, it makes me feel quite sick and it makes me go 'goosey' because it's such a horrible, horrible noise, it's the warning of fear, of danger coming to you.

I'm sure that if we hadn't gone there would have been a lot of people killed. There would have been a lot of my generation as we are now wiped out because the bombing in Hastings was horrific as was the bombing in London; where so many children died and lost their lives, so I think it was justified. If you manage to mention evacuation to people they've always got a good point to come up with, as well as a sad point, and I always think when I'm talking to them that they're different because the war and evacuation made them a different sort of person. I'm sure I'm more tolerant, through going through what I went through. I think it also makes you more thankful for things that surround you now; as well as the fact that it also makes you a bit bitter because it's awful to say but the younger people, so many of them, abuse what they've got these days. They have got so much to be thankful for and I think that is why the people who were evacuated have come back more gentle and more tolerant and more appreciative too of what they've got.

My religious faith was a very strict thing from my parents but perhaps strict is not the word, I was led by them not forced by them. It wasn't, "You will go to church today" or, "You will go to Sunday school". We were led to go and I think in time the leading came not from them but from the Lord, from our own faith, we just wanted to do it. My brother built a model church when he was about seventeen, he probably hasn't got it now but it was so beautiful. He took so many photographs of it; it looked like the interior of a church. It was built from everything he could get his hands on and he made a stained glass window with chipped bits of broken glass and he got someone with a lathe to make some teeny-weeny candle sticks. He made his own candles from running wax down. He's very clever with his hands.

We've been involved all our lives with the church. He went to Canterbury Cathedral as senior Vesturer (a keeper of vestments) in 1966. It was the year my mother died and he stayed there quite a while with them and then he had 'the call'. He'd wanted to be a clergyman all his life. He said to my dad, "I don't really want to work at Hollingsworth as a coach builder, I want to be a vicar." And my dad said, "We can't afford to send you to college". In those days there had to be college fees. He was ordained about 17 years ago so he got there in the end. He went to the Canterbury School of Ministry while he was working at the cathedral at the same time as senior Vesturer. My mother and father had died, so neither of them saw him ordained but it was a wonderful day that day and Dr Coggan was a good friend of his, he helped him so much by being at Canterbury.

I had a lot of problems in my own marriage; we went ten years before we had any children, and then my husband had a road accident and became a manic-depressive. Of course I had the two children and how do you keep children quiet when you've got a manic-depressive in the house? It was very, very difficult. My sister-in-law said to me, "One day when I open that door, you are going to be there with the two children". She said, "I'll take you in and you may make this your home." I thought that was a wonderful thing to say and I used to run away to Canterbury with the children time and time again when things got very bad. He didn't treat me badly, it's just that I couldn't understand why he was so depressed when he'd got not only me but two lovely children. I think it was because he had been involved in the war and he used to have very bad nights. He was in the Royal Marines, and the only thing he told me was that they came to somewhere in France in a flat-bottomed barge boat and that's all I ever knew. It must have been a terrifying experience; it might have been the Normandy landing. He used to have the most terrible nights and he would never, ever tell me what he dreamt about. I used to say, "Tell me what you're dreaming" "I can't, I can't" and he would go all hot and shaky. "Please tell me, if you tell me you'll get it off your mind and then I'll understand". "I don't want to tell you, I can't tell you." I think the accident triggered it off and brought it all back, what he'd been through in the war, the bad experiences.

When I've told other people, they say that reaction is the 'shell-shock'. They didn't know much about trauma in those days. It was very difficult; it was very hard to cope with, very hard. He died ten years ago. I had to go to have my blood pressure taken the other day. The nurse said to me, "How did you feel when your husband died?" I said, "Well obviously I was sad, but there was a strange feeling of relief." Now that can't be wrong. I said to the nurse, "That can't be wrong" It was just that he'd been relieved from his pain and his pain was dreadful because he would be awake all night and he would sleep all day because he didn't like the dark. He would not let me in, he wouldn't tell me; I couldn't help him. It was quite bad really, because when you think of it there's nothing worse than trying to help someone and you can't and I tried to help my brother so much and couldn't.

My brother visited recently and saw the tape of the Evacuees' Reunion Association service at Westminster Cathedral. He sat there and he just looked at that tape, then he looked straight at me and straight out of the window. And I thought 'pain', there's still a hurt there and he couldn't talk about it. I respected that. I thought it's no good saying to him, "Do you want to watch the tape?" or anything like that. Goodness me, Westminster was so emotional! I've never felt so emotional in all my life. When that Spitfire came over and everyone was cheering and clapping I was standing there crying. I thought the whole thing was the most emotional thing I've ever been through, it went so deep, it brought something that was deep inside out. It was a strange feeling, because we were all looking at each other, we were all sort of relating, it was a most peculiar feeling. I thought it was a beautiful service, Mr Roffey and all those that took part; Michael Aspel was there and the girl that sang brought back what we'd been through. You know I could see in a lot of those faces, in the faces of a lot of those other people, how I felt inside. I don't know what I looked like but I know I felt like some of those people looked, very deeply sad, but then there was a sort of joy, it was a sort of relief joy. When the Spitfire came over and we were all outside, I looked round and I thought, "Gosh, they're all, they're all clapping and cheering," but I was just a crying heap. It was a very profound experience; very strong feelings were released. You see I wanted to help my brother and I couldn't, I wanted to help my husband and I couldn't, because I couldn't get inside. I've got another dear friend, who's going through a 'sadness' and I cannot get inside of her.

It's a strange thing, isn't it, to have said all this and then to realise that this is probably what the war did. I wanted to help everyone, I wanted to take everyone round and say, "You're all going to be all right, everyone's going to be fine," because I wasn't the one that cried very often, everybody else seemed to cry but I was the one who said, "You're going to be fine. We'll all stick together and we'll all be safe". I suppose I was an optimist and hoped for the best. I didn't cry when I was away from my parents; only when the letters came and when they left at the end of their visits, I used to cry then. It may be it's sort of still there a bit and it comes out now because I'm a very, very emotional person, very emotional. I don't think I was emotional before but I am now, anyone can say the slightest thing to me now and I am hurt.

I've got a very good friend; she's been a good friend of mine for about fifty years, I rang her up about six o'clock one morning recently, when I was going through a bad time. She lives in Rye and is married to a chap who works in the Post Office. He used to go into a pub in Queens Road to have a drink with my husband and I used to go down there with him and that's how we met and she's Godmother to the children. I rang her up at six o'clock that morning crying and in a terrible state and she talked to me until nearly seven o'clock. She talked me through something that could have been horrible. Once, I went to counselling when I was a bit down over something, but I can't remember what that was about, so it can't have been anything very serious. But this last time when the doctor said to me, "Would you like to go to counselling?" I said, "No, I can do this myself." He said, "Are you sure?" and I said "Yes", and he gave me these dreadful pills and they were useless. I said, "I can do it without pills but I do want some pills to make me sleep". If I can sleep all night I can cope with the day. Oh I'm much better now, much better, but I just feel a bit fearful. I mean anything can go wrong and I'm very sensitive to what people say. I'm too sensitive, but I'm all right if I'm in control and I'm sure that has been brought on by going through the war.

## Chapter 8. 'The library was a form of escape from life.'

## Roy Judge's Story.

I'm Roy Edmund Judge aged seventy-one, born July 1929 to humble but worthy parents in London Road, St. Leonard's, at the home of some friends of my mother. I was the first child of two; my younger brother was born in 1934, David. We lived for a while on one of the hills, the East or West Hill, I always get confused in Hastings. The Judge family originated from the bakery at the bottom of the High Street where my grandfather had worked, but we'd really broken loose from the High Street Judges at this point in time and my grandfather was working in Catsfield as a baker. My father was working in Mumfords watchmakers in North Street at St Leonard's on Sea, a turning just off London Road. We had what was a sort of Grace and Favour house from the church in return for a bit of care-taking duties on the Gensing Road Institute, which wasn't directly associated with St Leonard's Parish Church, but indirectly I think it was part of their Evangelical arm. The Institute was not Church of England that was the point but the Rector of the very Evangelical Parish Church had some hold or importance in the running of the Institute. So my father as a member of the church choir and my mother as a member of the Mothers' Union were in as Caretakers. One of my earliest happy memories is of helping my father getting the hall, the rooms of the Institute, ready for the Choir Club and that sort of thing. It was a very strange house, this Caretaker's house. It was large, with four bedrooms upstairs and a kitchen and a scullery off it, a sitting room and then outside a couple of yards there was a biggish shed and 'outworks,' as it were, which my brother and I enjoyed very much. The area is now a conservation area and has distinctly gone 'up market' but at that time it was a nice ordinary working class, servant class area that serviced the bigger houses further up Pevensey Road. Lots and lots of little shops, you go out of the door and within a hundred yards you had everything that you needed down to newsagents; all sorts of interesting shops with interesting people. I could be sent out with a jug to get milk from the dairy from Chapman's, just across the road, and pop round the corner to a shoe-mender's or anything. Going to school simply meant going along streets to Mercatoria, you go up until you come to Mercatoria School.

I first went to school when my brother was born in 1934 when I was four and a half or so, and I felt that I was being rejected, a classic case. My parents were very sweet and I don't think it sank deeply into my psyche but I do remember hiding round the corner and not going off to school as one of my earliest memories. But I enjoyed school, very nice Miss Hatter with the infants, Miss Graham next class up; I can't remember the others. I just shot up because I was very capable and I could read before I went to school and I enjoyed school very, very much and just flourished in the atmosphere. I don't remember anything in particular going wrong; I just enjoyed it. I took the exam, the scholarship, you took a written and then the Oral, the Oral was an Intelligence Test. I don't remember the details, but anyway I passed at the age of ten. So I went to the Grammar School in '39 when I was just ten with three people from Mercatoria, feeling quite confident about school and everything and went into 2J. The first form were the boarders. I was in the top stream and I had no consciousness of any division at that time, but I was still coping quite happily, and my parents were very proud of me. My mother had been a Barnardo's child and she wanted the family to be a happy family and we were, very.

She had a very happy childhood because she was fostered by an elderly couple who took Barnardo's children and had done for years. She went there when she was two and stayed there until she was fourteen. She'd passed the scholarship exam but she couldn't take it up because Barnardo's children didn't take up scholarships, so she went back to Barnardo's Headquarters, Barkingside and was trained for Service. She used to tell stories of how she wept into the bucket as she was learning to scrub stairs, as she saw herself as a lost princess, that sort of thing, but she had this very happy marriage to my father who came from Hastings but was working in Blackheath, while she was in service.

By the time I went to the Grammar School she was taking in lodgers during the summer, because she'd got this biggish house and just the two children and so it was a very happy life. I went through the first year 1939 to '40 at the Grammar School very happily because I'd got many local friends in the neighbourhood, but then the evacuation came - July 21st 1940 - and we were sent off, it was all rather exciting. I remember standing at the bottom of London Road and my mother saying goodbye to me. I have in fact got the letter we all had to send back, I've still got mine, which is a nice piece of evidence of my placidity at that particular moment in time.

*"Fowey"*
*Green Lane*
*St Albans*
*Herts.*
*23-7-40.*

*Dear Mum,*

*This is just about the first opportunity I've had to write to you so I hope you are not worrying. I've got billeted in a very nice place, so please don't worry.*

*There is a dog at my billet but no children, and the jelly did go down well and I did have quite enough to eat.*

*We have joined the library here and I've just got a book out, which looks very good. We have also seen the museum (one of two) – the cathedral, which is very, very big and ghostly, the excavations (Roman) and the golf course, which is run by the town and bigger than the Hastings one by far.*

*Please could you send my bathing costume up.*

*Send my love to David, Daddy and Grand-dagh and if you write to aunt tell her that I'll be writing soon. I hope that David will like the Rupert and Dad the Greyfriars. But I have got to go out now so*

*Yours for ever lovingly*

*Roy.*

*xxxxxxxxxx*

So in 'the market' when we arrived at St Albans I was chosen by an elderly lady with a forty-year old daughter at home, and a husband who was getting on but still seemed quite active to me. He in fact died of heart trouble 1947 or so. He ran a music shop on Holywell Hill with his forty-year old daughter and she played something. They had two sons, one of whom was going to be part of a Royal Air Force band. I only remember vaguely because I didn't know him.

They were double-barreled. Mr C-S- played the organ at one of the St Albans churches but I never went there. Anyway they were a very nice couple with the one middle-aged daughter living at home. So I was taken off by this Mrs C-S-, whose Christian name was Hetty, I think. I don't remember mister's Christian name I don't think I ever knew it. There was some discussion as to what I was going to call her. She was very sweet, and she said, "Well you call your mummy, mummy, so you could call me mother perhaps." She obviously wanted to do the right thing and so I sort of gritted my teeth and said, "Well if you say so," and so I did, but I remember feeling a certain element of disloyalty at this point, but it didn't impinge terribly because they were very nice and obviously wanted to 'do me proud'.

They lived in a very nice bungalow, which I suspect had been the first building plot at the bottom of Green Lane. It was out near the golf course and The Ancient Britain pub, which was a bus stop. From The Ancient Britain there was this unmade up lane, it carried on as Everlasting Lane that went on to what was the Verulamium Road that carried you out of St Albans on the other side, so we were very much on the fringe of the city - out on the golf course sort of area. This bungalow was in large grounds and I was there four and a half years in the same billet. They must have had thirty or forty apple trees, and one of my jobs in the autumn was to pick the apples and to help to store them in straw. They'd got a garage and another biggish sort of outhouse with racks for storage. They'd got someone who was a family retainer who was rather a character. His trousers had a band at the knee and he used to come and do the garden and organise the picking and the storing of the fruit, and he gave me the freedom to take an apple when I came back from school, which was very nice. It was all very pleasant and when I was told how to mow the lawn I rather enjoyed just going round in circles, so that was happy.

I had to go to bed at nine o'clock. I suppose I worked up to nine o'clock but one thing that beats in my memory is the Lily Bolero tune. It was the introduction to the News and I was in bed by then. I had to go off early and everything was timed, very, very timed, very structured but not at all unhappy in any obvious sort of way. I was fed. I think she saved her beans until they were too chewy, which was a pity but I was fed and watered and I just read. I used to read walking to school and read on the way back, walking. When I came to where the 391 bus started, somewhere up there at the end of Union Lane, where the Workhouse was, as long as I had half an hour left I was all right: I could enjoy the walk, I was very solitary. There were other boys in the same class along the way but I didn't aim to meet anyone else, I was just me with my reading.

I can't stage the books that I read. I read one hundred and fifty E. Phillips Openheim and one hundred Edgar Wallace but I wasn't as keen on Richmal Compton as the other boys were. By the end of the time there I was certainly into crime fiction but not quite so keen on Agatha Christie. John Dixon Carr and Carter Dixon, who were actually the same person produced a lot. I still have the list of crime fiction books from my English master who was a lovely man but incapable of keeping discipline. He obviously saw me as being a hope for the future as someone who read. I remember him giving me a copy of Lamb's Essays, which I didn't particularly enjoy, but I must have written a nice essay about Charles Lamb whom he was very fond of. Almost certainly he was encouraging me in my interest, or trying to encourage me to read, but I was deeply into crime fiction and he was lovely in the fact that he didn't try to change me in any way.

It was all very idyllic at first, but the immediate problem was accommodation in school because we shared St Albans School which they had in the mornings and we had in the afternoons, or maybe it was the other way round. It was 'Cox and Box.' with interesting buildings on the edge of the Verulamium. But that first autumn I suppose we went straight away into our school pattern of being minded all the time and having a lot of free time down on Verulamium, quite idyllic, I just remember a lot of fine weather.

It was a disciplined school; there were four masters who had the ability to cane. The Head as one got to know him was a bit of a laughing stock really, M G G Hyder. He was a funny little man whose chief characteristic was to put words in the middle of other words in order to give them emphasis and I suppose he kept a hold on things but Stroob Baker, who was the senior master, was in charge and he was a disciplinarian. He ran the scouts and I suspect he'd got a soft spot for the boys but it didn't show, I certainly wasn't conscious of that. He was the rock on which I think the thing was based and he caned and you didn't want to be caned by him. You got caned for being late, which I think was the only reason I was ever caned.

Then Miller, Nick Miller, who was a lovely man, took French; he could cane but he didn't like hurting people so it was minimal. I remember Rushby Smith caning; perhaps they all caned but there were obviously restraints on this, so you didn't get a feeling of general terror, but certain masters lost their temper. Mr Pearce was the one who we didn't enjoy terribly, he taught Latin and children couldn't remember Latin. He would throw books at one and he would get really terribly cross, terribly cross. He was obviously a sensitive soul really, because he was Plymouth Brethren. We used to see him going to the little chapel and they were very separatist and very 'what have you' and he was 'one of them'. I suspect that that would explain a lot; it was a very black and white denomination. I didn't ever know him as a person and didn't come to terms with him, didn't ever have to, but he was just not cut out for teaching.

Some of the other members of staff were lovely. Bill Rees, doing history... oh a wonderful man! He was Welsh; he committed suicide in the end which was very strange, I never could understand that, because he was delightful and one of the chief reasons why I went on to do history. Then there was Bill Barnett who we regarded as a hypocrite; we had a very low opinion of him. The younger members of staff went off to the war, people like Tom Cookson, the one who married Catherine. I'd had him for Chemistry. He went off, but then came back in the sixth form, I knew him quite well. Mr Lawrence, 'Annie Laurie', was a fascinating man. I remember having him for English and he was a very nice man. Mr Ryan was a very interesting man, very colourful. I always thought that he must have had another slice of life, as it were, that he must be famous for something else and that I'd 'turn him up' somewhere but he went off to the war. Mr Bowmer was younger but he stayed, he may have had something wrong with him but he did the sport and was a bit of a softie really but we liked him, so they were a bit of a mixture. Tosser Wright was dapper and he taught Latin quite well - I enjoyed it, or was it just that I enjoy patterns of words? Anyway, I passed and went on to do it at A level at Higher Schools Certificate. I was very peaceful when we'd settled down. You see a lot of people left and we became quite small classes but there were some people who kept moving billets and there were some people who were obviously unhappy, but I was all right.

(Roy with the headmaster behind him in 1940, he has his gas mask held by a lead round his neck.)

We were housed, I think for two consecutive years, in the Abbey Institute, which was just off Holywell Hill and obviously associated with the Abbey; we'd got some rooms in there and I remember the sun shining through the window because I had a desk by the window. I had a 'pecking order' and could get the desk I wanted by Machiavellian means because being small and insignificant I had to make my mark by humour rather than by sporting prowess. I certainly wasn't sporting at all but I can remember just luxuriating in that sun and seeing butterflies. The staff never used to come because they were going from one building to another and we were the 'all right' class because we were the A stream, so we'd just be set some work.

My parents stayed in Hastings briefly, I suppose. My aunt Connie was the only other member of our extended family, apart from my grandfather, because my grandmother had died before my parents married, of TB. My aunt had taken a job as a maid at Uplands School, a Church of England Public Girls School in St Leonard's, which was evacuated to Aberystwyth, to a large house requisitioned for schools which had been the home of Lady Rolls of Rolls Royce. So aunt Connie was down there with Uplands School, and my mother went with her and worked as a maid and took David my brother, which was disastrous for him really. It must have been very, very traumatic because effectively he was starting school at five. His school was in the village and the house where they lived with my aunt had a two-mile drive and it was a long walk. It was a Welsh-speaking area so he just clammed up. I remember going down there for Christmas.

My father had found himself a job in Barnet; he could get a job very easily as a watchmaker, and he'd gone to London to be more accessible to me, (Barnet is at the end of the Northern Line on the Underground). He had to leave my grandfather in Hastings because he refused to move. He took me down to Wales that first Christmas and I remember the journey with him quite vividly because I would have been ten, just the sheer excitement of this long train journey. We kept having to stop and start again from sidings and this sort of thing, it must have been so tedious but quite exciting to a ten-year-old, and then going to this big house where my mother and my aunt were senior members of the sizeable servants' hall. I vividly remember that I was reading Mark Twain at the time 'A Tramp Abroad' and realising how funny it was. She said, "Stop laughing boy" because I was upsetting the servants' hall and I just couldn't stop reading or stop laughing. Mum felt that I was being rude (which I probably was) and she was embarrassed by this awful habit I had of showing off. I'd earned myself a very bad reputation in Sunday school; I was a very good boy all the rest of the time but in Sunday school I knew that I was 'top dog' and that I would get a good mark, there's this 'other side' of me you see, who on the face of it just couldn't say 'boo to a goose'. It was the 'phoney war' time, so soon after that my mother and my brother came back to Hastings and my brother went to West St Leonard's School, which was the only primary school open. They stayed there for the rest of the war and I went back for holidays after that first Christmas. Every holiday I went back to Hastings with all the other horde of Grammar School boys who were going back, and there were always a lot of us. We had two ways of going, either by bus to Barnet and then Northern line or by train to King's Cross and I remember getting quite expert on how you crossed London when I was ten.

I really wasn't conscious of the war. There was the one bomb on St Albans down on the golf course, and one could see the lights from London burning but I was never conscious of anything there or while I was in Hastings. I was conscious of the atmosphere of war; the tank traps and the barbed wire on the front and this sort of thing and using the Morrison shelter and at a slightly later stage going down to Marina Court to sleep in their cellars where people had their own pitches. My parents went down there for a while, and when I was at home I went with them but my grandfather never ever stirred from home and we didn't have any bombs in our 'neck of the woods' except something in Gensing Road! I'm sure it was a 'doodlebug' and I was worried for my parents, but my father quickly returned to Hastings. My mother and my brother had gone back, partly because my aunt had now resigned from the school and had joined the Land Army as an assistant warden at a hostel in Markyate, just north of St Albans, specifically with the idea of keeping an eye on me, which was very nice because I could get the bus out to Markyate, which is a village half way between St Albans and Luton. The house that the Land Army had taken over was called Cheveralls, it had belonged to the Seabrights, a landed family; my aunt was an assistant warden there. She had been born in 1908 so she was in her early forties and seeing life for the first time really, it was wonderful for her. I used to go and see her, trot over for weekends. The warden had a son who was about my age but I don't know that we did anything much together, I used to go and read. It was always one of my aunt's favourite stories that when I arrived on foot from Markyate, Mrs Haven who used to wait for me with her would say, "Connie, he's just walked by the gate." I was sort of reading you see, I'd walk along this country road always immersed in my book.

So it was nice that I'd kept those contacts with the family both in school holidays and with aunt Connie out at Markyate, where she stayed right through the whole time; it helped me not to feel terribly bereft, and I was coping quite happily at school. I remember the teachers fighting over me. Mr Baker the maths chap said at St Albans, "What are you going to do in the sixth form?" and I said, "Well, I suppose I'm going to do history, French and English" and him saying, "Oh, I thought you were going to do maths", he obviously saw me as a mathematician, which was rather flattering, but I felt I was doing better at history, English, French and Latin I suppose.

Every Sunday church was compulsory, and I remember collecting the Sunday Express for my foster parents, I would do that but I had no social life. I even remember playing 'hookey' from the British Restaurant where we had to go to for lunch but I didn't like the food there, so I went and bought rolls at a baker's and didn't go. Someone picked up on this and I had to be checked in, so that was a sign of a bit of rebellion but very, very slight, my rebellion was utterly, utterly minimal. I spent all my time in the library, making friends with the librarians from age eleven to fifteen. I didn't feel I was missing my home life at all. My mother was so good too at missing me but not missing me too much. She came up for some weekends, I remember meeting her, and she got a bit weepy but very sweet... no more that one should. The Public Schools do this as a matter of course: it isn't an unusual event to be bereft of your children and it was what had to be, so she accepted it. She obviously felt that I was in good hands and she accepted it. She was so good when I went off to University too, when you recall there was no telephonic communication and she was really losing me. Then I married a girl from Tilbury, which for her was the end of the earth but she did just the right things.

I obviously did go in on myself with all the reading. I don't know that I would have read only crime fiction if I'd had more intelligent conversation to urge me on, I had nothing to spur me on. Peter C- and myself got to know each other during our GSC (General Schools Certificate) years. We did a lot of identifying of questions and working out of material, especially with the Latin. We made lists of conjugations and declensions for each other and I remember playing a kind of Bridge for two with Peter; we got it out of a book of card games.
When we got back we had the Philosophical Society, which was started by Mr Conisby the English teacher who took an interest in me, saw me as a lover of Lamb that sort of thing. He wanted to restart the glory days of the Philosophical Society, which he remembered from before the war, so he encouraged Peter and myself. I was the secretary and Peter was the publicity manager and we tried to get all the sixth form to come to the meetings after the return from St Albans. The return was fine: I was so pleased to get back because Peter and I were just fed up; Peter had been in the same billet like me the whole time. I was just bored with it, probably because nothing much happened; certainly nothing against the foster parents. We just wanted to get back to ordinary life and it seemed such a waste of time, well learning time as it were. I think we felt we could do it more efficiently at home but we both did reasonably well at General Schools Certificate. No, I think it was the direction of the reading, the library centeredness of it. Peter was very proud that he'd only read five books, two of which were the GSC set books. He saw himself as a mathematician, a logician and a rational thinker; we were a very nice pair when you look back on it. I saw myself as a reader I

think... just reading, but reading with a slight difference. I discovered a

Roy in the 6<sup>th</sup> form.
3<sup>rd</sup> row back, 3<sup>rd</sup> from the right.

book by Holbrook-Jackson called The Anatomy of Bibliomania. It was a large sized, antique volume that I don't suppose anyone else had ever taken out. I can remember its position on the shelf. I used to hide books behind others if I wanted to save them and was already using all my tickets although I'd got fifteen tickets. I read Bibliomania but I don't think I understood it, it was probably a 'take off' on a 17th Century author whose name I've forgotten; it was pseudo.

Holbrook Jackson I know now was a writer in the nineties and in the pre World War. I'd like to know more about him because he said some interesting things about the 1890's, but he's quite irrelevant. I wasn't aware then of Holbrook Jackson as a person, all I was aware of was that this was a nice high-sounding word that I could use to impress my friends you see. I wanted the reputation of being a knowledgeable 'literary orator' or something - not that I would have expressed it in that way. The library was a form of escapism from life it was my shield against... well, that's a very interesting question. I certainly wasn't unhappy in the library, I certainly wasn't unhappy outside the library. I'd still got to walk along Union Lane reading my books, so that was still almost extended library. I don't know that I was escaping any more than my friends were escaping by playing football. I don't know if I would have been like this at home. I certainly wouldn't have shared it with my parents; my unformed sort of amorphous, or whatever it was; the unformed 'undirectedness' of the interest in the Anatomy of Bibliomania, the liking of long words for themselves.

At fifteen, when I went back to Hastings in the sixth form I did mature, going on to read Virginia Woolf and Dostoevski and that sort of thing, when I was aware that these were the right things to read. I think it took me a long time to read them and I wasn't sure what I was getting out of them and yet obviously I was fighting my way through and, goodness me! , I didn't understand Virginia Woolf; so I gave up on her.... . I think it was 'The Waves and The Years'; they obviously weren't the right thing to be reading at that age or something. Dostoevsky and The Brothers Karamazov, I did get something from that but it took me an awful long time. I read Ulysees a couple of years ago to accompany radiotherapy and I know that I did that much more systematically and got a lot more out of it. It was the right way to do it, but whether that was because I was sixty-nine, rather than fifteen, I don't know.

Whether I would have done better with a bit more pointed guidance, I don't know. I remember again in the sixth form the Divinity teacher had come back from the war, he was a very nice man but a failed priest. He didn't really know what he believed... bless him. He'd gone into Divinity teaching because he knew about theology but he hadn't got his own life sorted out; which was not a bad thing really, for that lesson. But he got us all to try to tackle a Divinity prize essay 'What I Believe' was the subject and I think he only got one entry from me and I'm not sure if I've still got that. I was obviously brought up in a very religious atmosphere and the church youth club was certainly going after the war. My friend Joyce and I were both reacting against the black and white Evangelical fundamentalist flavour of the Parish church in a very unkind sort of way. We realised that these were nice people who meant well but we just didn't like their way of expressing it. It wasn't until I got to the University and realised that there was an alternative, you know the Student Christian Movement sort of approach, the Liberal Anglican approach that didn't have to have it so black and white. So I rather saw what I believe as in negative terms 'I can't accept this'. It's very difficult to crystallise what you believe in, I... still can't.

I expect the war itself and evacuation had a great effect on my philosophy of life - I'm sure it would have done - but I can't remember a single influential person or book, except the Anatomy of Bibliomania, which was really just symbolic in a sense. All the people that I do remember that I wanted to copy came along later. The war obviously had impact by evacuation; it's a backcloth I think, I've always enjoyed pattern. It was the reason I went on to read so many E. Phillips Openheim and filled in the gaps in my English teacher's chart of crime authors in that year, it was the challenge of filling the pattern and completing the sequence, which has always appealed to me, gathering the facts. That was my line, hiding the books in the library so that I could come back to them because of the war; there was just me, as it were, being enabled to do my thing but not a thing that one would be terribly proud of, but I then went on to use libraries well. I remember how impressed Mr Conisby was by an article I produced for the Philosophical Society but I didn't tell him I'd lifted most of it from this book in the library. Well, I think I did tell him, and he said, "Never mind, selection doesn't matter, it doesn't matter, the art of pulling out and selecting material is good in itself".

Roy back home in Hastings.

So perhaps all this 'laying fallow' was all right. I certainly didn't feel deserted by my family, no I didn't; bless them because they made a point of keeping contact. When I went back I couldn't relate to my brother as well as I should have done, but then you see I went to University and he didn't, I think because he had missed out on schooling by staying at home and he hadn't got the confidence that I'd got with exams at that stage. But it was also that I was eighteen and he was fourteen, it's a bad age gap unless you've built up a lot and he had got different friends: and then he emigrated to Canada. He went into Smiths, the bookshop; he was selling them not reading them. I've got five grandchildren and he's got four grandchildren, we're quite good in the family stakes, just separated by the Atlantic, the family remains intact. I'd had fun until ten... I can't think... and I used to come home for holidays and I think we still did fun holidays. My happy memories were of going up to Ecclesbourne with my family as a regular thing; going out to North Seat and we still did that. There are pictures extant... patterns of an ongoing family tradition and I carried on reading funny books you see, reading Mark Twain when I can't have been more than eleven, then I entered this other world of reading of detective books... patterns... that's right. Looking at my understanding of human nature and disagreements that lead to war, I'm just horrified by the way in which they build up but I don't know that I thought about it. It's the 'them and us' situation that creates power struggles and misunderstandings.

# Roy's Obituary

WHEN TENNYSON entered the Sheldonian Theatre in Oxford to accept an honorary degree, the august occasion was abruptly deflated by a cry from the gallery, "Did your mother call you early, Mr Tennyson?", in allusion to the famous line in his poem The May Queen.

Roy Judge's animated description of the occasion, in a talk about May Day given at the Calendar Customs conference in 1984, had his audience in fits of laughter while simultaneously imprinting on their minds several of the crucial elements in his approach to folk studies: how custom can be informed by art and literature, how our response to customary activities is shaped by our cultural baggage, and how – as with any historical discipline, but neglected by folklorists of the past – we need to return to the primary sources to illuminate our understanding of what is happening. In the case of The May Queen, Judge had returned to the local newspapers and diarists of the poet's childhood home in Lincolnshire to answer the question, "Was Tennyson writing of what he had seen, or what he had read?"

Roy Judge was born in Hastings in 1929 and attended its grammar school, though for much of that pe-

Judge: Merrie England

riod the school was evacuated to St Alban's. It was there that he developed a voracious reading habit which helped him towards a place at Oxford to read History in 1947. At Oxford he met his future wife Betty Jones, and was pleased when his National Service posting to Cowley Barracks enabled the relationship to flourish. They married in 1954.

His initial career was in teaching: he spent five years in Peckham and then, after completing a Diploma in Religious Studies, five at Erith

tory and later religious studies. By that time he was an active morris dancer with both the London Pride team and – as a graduate of Oxford – the Ancient Men, the name adopted by Oxford University Morris Men on tour. His dancing with the latter group saw him perform, over the years, everywhere from America to Estonia and Japan. These annual tours took time, and he seized the opportunity to move to the post of lecturer in religious studies at Furzedown Training College, in London, where the longer vacations afforded more time for dancing.

Judge's innovative and influential work in folk studies began only in the second half of his life. His first published study of custom was for Folk Music Journal in 1971, commemorating the beginnings of the folk dance revival in Oxford 60 years before. Three years later he took a sabbatical from Furzedown, ostensibly to broaden his skills into social anthropology, but combining work and pleasure by pursuing research into the Jack-in-the-Green, that walking bush which in past days paraded the streets in the company of sweeps on May Day.

Earlier, more romantic writers had mixed the Jack with the mediaeval foliate head and Green Man, but Judge sought instead the historical records and contemporary accounts of the custom, and showed (in The Jack-in-the-Green: a May Day custom, 1979) its origin in the 18th and development in the 19th centuries into the form in which it captured folklorists' attention in the 20th.

This work was recognised as breaking new ground in folk research. Judge followed it with a series of studies – including a doctoral dissertation – focused around the concepts of May Day, morris dancing and Merrie England. He unearthed, and analysed in meticulous detail, a wide variety of primary source material from newspaper accounts and playbills to village school records. At the same time he used literary and artistic sources to show how high culture mediated traditional custom, in some cases reinvented it, and in the end, through its quest for roots and authentic recreation, rediscovered how the ordinary people of England actually used to celebrate, dance and sing.

Typical was his work on the Victorian pageant master D'Arcy Ferris, who revived the "Shakespearean" Bidford morris in 1886.

Going beyond the material in libraries and archives, he traced Ferris's descendants, discovered that they still possessed Ferris's own splendid scrapbook of photographs, letters and cuttings relating to his extravaganzas, and persuaded the family to give him access to the material. His success in this was due, as much as anything to his remarkably pacific and congenial character. He was infinitely kind and patient with all he met, characteristically heaping blessings upon the good and extending sympathetic understanding to the incompetent and the bad.

Roy Judge was not one to seek advancement – he retired early in 1980 and devoted his time to research without any formal position – but found himself President of the Folklore Society from 1990 to 1993, and in the last year of his life was awarded both its Coote Lake medal and the gold badge of the English Folk Dance and Song Society.

MICHAEL HEANEY

Roy Edmund Judge, historian and folklorist: born Hastings, Sussex 2 July 1929; married 1954 Betty Jones (two sons, one daughter); died London 17 November 2000.

'The Independent' December 2000.

## Chapter 9. 'We saw the bomb drop just outside the window.'

### Pricilla's Story

When the war started I was at the High School and living at home with my mother, father and brother who was three years younger. My father's mother and father lived in Clive Vale and I had an aunt locally. We were just an ordinary working class family. My father would go fishing in his boat, not for a living but to help out; it was quite tough but we had enough.

I remember the war starting; we were in our back garden when I heard the siren going. I started at the High School just after that and the evacuees from London were coming to our school; they had to have half a day in church halls and half a day in our school; we didn't have any in our house. I can't remember my parents telling us we were going to be evacuated at all and when we went it felt like we were going on holiday and would come back in a couple of months. I do remember going on the train and having no idea where we were going to, with instructions from my mother to keep with my brother at all times. We got on well together and he wasn't a naughty boy because my parents were very strict and had brought us up to behave in other people's homes. The first thing that happened when we got to Ware was that he went to one billet and I went to another, I can't remember how I felt about it but somehow or other within a few days he came and lived with me.

Although we had been sent away to be in a safe place there were air raids going on at Ware when we arrived, and within a few days of my brother coming to live with me a bomb dropped two doors away from us and killed seven people, the noise was tremendous. Then another bomb dropped outside our window in the garden, - it was an oil bomb that threw black substance everywhere but luckily it didn't ignite. My foster parents didn't have a shelter. When the siren went we had gone downstairs to the lowest room in the house and we saw the bomb drop just outside the window, of that room... we saw it. The gas mantle fell off in the blast and floated across the room leaving us in darkness; the blast also locked all the doors in the house so there we were shut in, in the dark, waiting for someone to come and force the doors open to get us out.

First of all we were taken to an air raid shelter at a church down the road from us where we were looked after, we then went to the billet where my brother had been previously, but I can't remember what happened to the people where the bomb fell. These foster parents that had originally taken my brother were an elderly couple who had never had any children of their own, so they didn't really understand us but they coped with us in their tiny two up and two down cottage with a toilet just outside the back door. I shared a room with my brother who seemed to be all right and we both went to school. Our school shared Ware Grammar School for half the day and the other half we spent in church halls, just like it had been for St Ursula's at Hastings. It was our turn now, and of course it would have been a better education if we had had a full day at school but I was in the Hockey Team and we played the Blue Coat School from Hertford sometimes.

The elderly foster parents we lived with had a niece living next door with children and other relatives in Ware with families who we saw sometimes, so we did mix with younger people whilst we were there but the gentleman became so ill after two or three months that our foster mother had to spend all her time looking after him and couldn't cope with us any more. My mother had come up to Ware after the bombing whilst we were with this elderly couple and I presume she got a domestic job where she could live in, but she wasn't happy being away from Hastings, so she didn't stay very long about three months I think, - then she went back.

When we left that billet my brother was separated from me again but he didn't stay there long, he wasn't happy at the next place. I think he found it tough being on his own and although it was a very nice house the lady took in working people as well. One man was doing night duty, so he slept in the daytime and worked at night, which meant he had the bed during the day and my brother had it at night. I don't think my mother liked the idea of that very much, and it was around the time when she was going back to Hastings, so she took my brother back with her and I stayed on.

I had a friend who was living at the vicarage; she had an evacuee friend with her who also went back to Hastings, so I was able to go there in her place. I had been brought up Church of England, so it was all right for me to live at the vicarage. I stayed there about eighteen months, and I was confirmed whilst I was there. They didn't have any children. The vicar's wife had a big house in the country that she had to lend to the Army for the girls in the Army who became pregnant. I don't know if they were allowed to keep their babies or not but we did go there sometimes to pick gooseberries in the big garden, it was always only to pick gooseberries. There was a maid, a cook and a gardener at the vicarage and we ate with them in their big kitchen during the week, and at the weekends we ate with the vicar and his wife. It was a beautiful house; I suppose we were lucky to live in a nice place like that, we were treated well by all of them there. The cook took our sugar ration because she had a lot of people to feed, so I gave up sugar there but we were given a bit on our porridge.

When my mother got back to Hastings she started a new job in the Land Army because most women had to do some sort of war work, she loved that. I think by then my brother did find a school he could attend. Mum worked in a Nursery and couldn't come and see me but she phoned me sometimes, which was a great luxury and I think I went home for holidays because I can't remember any Christmases away from home. I never saw my father all that time, though, because he was in the Air Force in India and couldn't get back to see us.

I don't remember missing my mum during that time, and my brother had gone home so I wasn't responsible for him any more. I'd known the friend I was billeted with from the age of seven, and when her mum and dad came up they would take me out with them. After the vicarage I went to another billet, this time it was an ordinary terraced house but I adapted again as children do, there was a husband and wife who had a daughter and a little boy. By this time I'd taken my exams, my School Certificate, but the results didn't come through until September and I'd gone home to Hastings by then. I'd achieved four credits and a pass; which was enough to get me into the Civil Service later, so I suppose the education at Ware couldn't have been too bad. I didn't need to take the Civil Service exam and stayed there for eleven years in a senior post over older people who were held back. When I first went back to Hastings I had to get a job and became a probationer telegraphist, they took me on trust, anticipating exam results.

We lived in Barley Lane, which had a mobile gun placement. The war was still on and we saw it in use during the time of the doodlebugs. At Ware we were so close to London that we knew when it was being bombed and could see the fires burning. My brother was left with a lasting impression after the bomb near us at Ware, he was nervous of noise, but it hasn't affected me in the long term. Another thing was that when my father returned from India we had a very difficult time because my mother had got used to running the house and doing everything, she was so independent; a different woman to the one he had married. They found it hard to re-adapt, also it was difficult for him to get used to us after we'd been separated for three years. Of course, as a child, it was not easy to realise what was going on, but looking back I can see how hard it must have been for everyone.

Of course the war had been a bit easier for me than for my brother because I was that bit older and I was lucky in the billets I went to because I was well looked after; I know some people weren't so lucky. I got married in 1950 and adopted a daughter in 1959 and I still live in Hastings.

## Chapter 10. 'I ate in the kitchen...they ate in the lounge.'

### Ellen's Story

My maternal grandparents lived in a tithe cottage called Century Cottage in Stowupland near Stowmarket in Suffolk. My grandfather was a farm manager, which was quite a good job, and they were fairly comfortably off, my grandmother was a midwife for the little village. My grandfather had his favourite horse and was out riding when the horse threw him, not intentionally, and my grandfather was kicked in the head and he subsequently died from that, so they had to leave the cottage and I remember my mother telling me how sad they all were at losing the employment of this very good landowner and the friendship of the daughter of the house Topsy. Shortly after that my mother went nursing. On my father's side my grandfather was born in Jersey, and one thing I remember hearing about him was that he had a very good singing voice, and was a choirboy in the church where Lily Langtree was married, and he sang at her wedding. After his marriage my grandfather came to London to find employment and did some sort of fine artwork by restoring pictures. They were both very religious people and my father's sister lived with them all their lives, she had a very good job in the Post Office. They both died during the war, and I was able to go to their funerals.

I lived in Hastings with my parents and my brother Ned, who is two years older than me. My father had a furniture removing business, he employed one other person to work with him on his van and two more men to work on another one he owned. So it was a comfortable, well-run business, but unfortunately when the war came the army commandeered his pantechnicons and as no one wants to be moving during war his business just folded up, so he then joined the Civil Defence and became an Air Raid Warden. My mother was a trained nurse and she used to do private work for Doctor Carpenter who lived next door to us. In the summer she let out three bedrooms for Bed and Breakfast, which I really enjoyed because I used to take the breakfast in and think I was the 'bee's knees' doing that, but it all came to an end when the war came. Just before the war my brother was very seriously ill with double pneumonia and Doctor Carpenter was really marvellous, and as he lived next door he was in and out all the time. I can remember the terrible words 'it's the crisis tonight'. Fortunately my brother got over it because it was before M&B and antibiotics or penicillin, so my mother really nursed him through it very well. It did of course leave him with a weak chest and he had to go to an Open Air School for a short time.

I was ten when war broke out and still in the junior school; after Dunkirk we were told we were going to be evacuated and were issued with gas masks, it was a week before my eleventh birthday and we went on July 21st 1940. I felt quite excited when we were going away in this train, we had no idea where we were going; we ended up in a little village four miles from Stevenage in Hertfordshire. We went to the church hall and I don't remember being picked out or anything, but I landed with this family called the Andrews.

My foster father was a farm worker and I felt rather sorry for him because he was a diabetic. I was always interested in nursing even in those days and I thought he was marvellous when he injected himself twice a day with insulin. He used to swear the whole time he was doing it, but as I watched him plunging the needle into his arm I felt he was quite brave. He was a pleasant person really, except that he did swear so, so did Mrs Andrews. She was a motherly sort and she worked hard by taking in washing to make a living, so I think she thought I would help the family and do quite a bit of the housework.

Renee, the eldest girl, was in service in a big house in the village as a Nanny, then there was Bill who was eighteen, I adored him, he was called up into the Navy, and I used to enjoy it when he came home on leave. There was another son Ken who went into the Army, and I liked him as well. The youngest was a girl, she was a couple of years younger than me and they called her Girlie but her real name was Diana. I shared her bedroom and she always wanted to sleep in bed with me. Her mother kept saying she wasn't to but when she begged me, really begged me to come in I let her. In the morning I was soaking wet from head to foot with urine. I thought, "Oh my goodness, I've wet myself, I can't possibly have done," but it was Girlie. It was horrid; I can still feel it now. Of course my bed wasn't prepared for it but Girlie's was, with mackintoshes and goodness knows what. Mrs Andrews wasn't too happy with me because it meant my bed was soiled, the mattress and so forth. She was never allowed in my bed again.

There are some things I like to remember about this little village. The school said that we must go to church on a Sunday morning, but we had to wait outside while the lady of the manor Miss Cotton-Brown arrived in her Daimler. As the chauffeur opened the door she swept in past us evacuees and we were instructed to curtsey, but I didn't. At Christmas time she invited us up to her Hall and gave us 'poor evacuees' a Christmas Tree and we were told to say, "Thank you very much Miss Cotton-Brown". I was allowed to go and help the farmer milk his cows on a lovely farm near where I lived. We got on very well and I really enjoyed that, working there in the summer. In the village, we used to have Beetle Drives and I've loved Beetle Drives ever since. There was a lot going on in the church as well, and it was a village with a very nice community spirit.

We all had to go to the church hall on a Saturday afternoon to write home to our parents. Our letters were then censored and if we said we were not happy we were called over and it was spoken about, and we had to rephrase it but I never put down that I was unhappy, because I was always quite happy with life. The teachers posted the letters, put the stamps on and posted them, so that they knew once a week our parents received a letter from us. I think it was a good idea and it stood me in good stead because I like writing letters now, but I can remember some of the children saying they were unhappy and they were called out and had to replace that bit. I suppose it should have been left in, but as I wasn't unhappy I didn't bother too much about it at the time.

My father came to see me when I'd only been there about six weeks or so, with about four of the parents, I think they must have come by taxi because no one had a car and in any case there wouldn't have been any petrol. They must have paid for someone to bring them; there was just one parent for each child, not both. I was so worried in case my foster parents swore but they never did and I was quite relieved. Strangely the one time when I quite blithely came out with a swear word at the table I was told, "Don't you ever let me hear you say that again," and I was really taken aback.

They proved to be a united sort of family. I was quite horrified when the eldest daughter came home and we were told that she was expecting a baby, of course she wasn't married. It was the first time I'd ever heard of anyone having a baby and not being married, so it was a bit of a shock to me and I didn't ever tell my parents that. No, I wasn't going to tell them that Renee's had a baby, but they all thought it was marvellous. They allowed her to stay on in the big house, being a nanny to their own child and bringing up her own baby, she took the baby to her job sort of thing. She never married the chap, I think she knew who it was but she didn't marry him. I can remember being quite horrified at all this, I suppose I was a bit prudish in my young way, really. It was a nice little baby and when she brought it to the house she often used to bring the other child who she was looking after as well. A lot of fuss was made of the little girl as well as the new baby but I remember being so taken aback when she wasn't married. I had to work hard myself and start the day by getting up early in the morning to light the fire, which was something I'd never done before in my life, but that was no bad thing for me really.

After I'd been there eighteen months I passed the 'eleven plus' but I didn't go to the High School, I went to where the Secondary school was, the Hastings Central School. I was told I was going to Welwyn Garden City and there I went. It was near my mother's younger sister; four stops on a little branch line, Harpenden in Hertfordshire. I was able to go and see my aunt and stay there about once a month, which was really very nice, and I got to know my cousins well. One was in the Merchant Navy, another in the Navy, and a girl cousin about my age, with whom I'm still very friendly.

At Welwyn Garden City I was billeted with very middle class people. I'm not sure what the husband did, but he was something in the city, a 'reserved' job, so he travelled there every day. He was a very pleasant man who would have loved children, but his wife did not like children and made it quite plain that she didn't like me, but the man was so kind he just made up for it really. She was a bit of a strange person, one of those who's always having headaches, an artistic type who loved ballet and loved music and, although she was an interesting sort of person, she did not like children but had to have me because they had a spare bed. But the man helped me with my homework, and I think he taught me a lot and built up my character, I feel that I owe him because he suggested books that I should read and gave me books, very good classical books, for my birthday and Christmas and I feel that he was an influence on my life.

They weren't religious at all, but I went to church, I went to the Free Church actually because that was the nearest. I would love to have been a Guide but they hadn't got any Girl Guides. I was a Brownie before I was evacuated and I would have 'flown' up to the Guides but because of evacuation I couldn't. They had the Girls Life Brigade in Welwyn Garden City, which I joined but I didn't like it so much somehow. They didn't mind me going to these things; they just left me quite a lot to my own devices, I think, looking back on it. Well they knew when I was going to the GLB but they didn't seem to be too interested in what I was doing. The foster father was interested in me when I was in the home but when I used to go to another girl's house I don't know if they knew where I was, but on the whole, he was interested in what I was doing I suppose but he was a very busy man because he was 'doing' the city; it was a very hush, hush business.

It was strange, because I was never allowed into their sitting room where they had a canary. I could hear this canary singing away but I never actually saw it behind the door, the door was never really open, so I never went into the sitting room. Mrs Hobbs was a bit 'off hand'. She wasn't unkind but I was a bit of a hindrance really, she didn't want me there, but I let it rub off because he was kind and helpful and taught me quite a bit. I used to help him in the garden stringing up his sweet peas and runner beans and I learned a lot from him; he would have gained a lot from having children of his own. He compensated for her. She seemed to leave most of the feeding of me to her poor husband. He always got my breakfast, which was Shredded Wheat and hot milk and for ages later in life I couldn't eat Shredded Wheat because I didn't have much milk and it was so cloying in my mouth. Shredded Wheat was made in Welwyn Garden City and if you went to the factory you could get misshapen boxes, which I would be sent to collect. He got up early to see me off to school and then went to London. When he came home at about 5.00pm he'd get my tea and I'd wash up. I always had a midday meal at school and then I just had a tea, which Mr Hobbs used to get. Of course I immediately had to get on with my homework every night, then I went to the GLB on Saturdays; I was never really out in the evenings. Sunday I always went to church, which I enjoyed.

He was quite a good cook really, and always prepared all the meals at the weekend. I used to help him peel the potatoes and carrots and things like that but I always ate the meal by myself, but I didn't mind, I just accepted that because I think fundamentally perhaps she wasn't very well. She was always tired and I think she was a bit anaemic because she looked so pale and he and I accepted that she wasn't a well person. I ate by myself in the kitchen-dining room, where I did my homework; they ate in the lounge, the place that I never went into but I didn't mind, I just had to accept it. It didn't make me unhappy there because there was only the three of us, but had the foster father been off hand as well then I would have been. He was such a pleasant person; he was always joking about this and that and always had a lovely smile on his face in contrast to his wife who never looked happy. Obviously looking back on it, she must have been an ill person and didn't, as I say, like children and didn't want children and then had to have me, an evacuee. They were forced to take me, I believe, by the Billeting Officer who went round there and found a spare bed.

Years later when I visited them after I had become a nurse, I was invited into the sitting room. I did invite them to my wedding but they were elderly then and couldn't come. They have since died. I used to get Christmas cards but they were mainly from the foster father really. I just accepted that the foster mother did not like children and she didn't go out much and always had a very pale complexion, she'd be lounging I think on the chaise-longue if there was one. I don't know how the housework was done; I didn't have to do any housework there. It was certainly a change from the first billet but I was that much older and I suppose expected to be a bit more mature. It was marvellous, being able to go over to Harpenden and see my aunt, my mother's younger sister, who was a great cook and it was very nice to have those lovely home made meals. Once I had a terrible sty in my eye and my foster mother said, "Well you just bathe it". Of course for a thirteen-year-old, it's a bit difficult bathing your eye. But my aunt, she very lovingly bathed it the whole weekend, I can remember now the soothing touch and it got better. I was rather, I suppose, left to my own devices but I don't think it did me any harm it made me stand on my own two feet.

The war hadn't finished when we came back, but gradually children were coming back to Hastings and leaving school. I'm not sure whether it was deemed that we should return by the authorities, but I remember going home. By that time I was fifteen and had left school. My parents wanted me to stay on at school but I couldn't, not at the Central School so I went for a year to Barton private school at St Leonard's. My mother knew the headmistress there and that's where I took my School Certificate. My mother had been called up, believe it or not, as a nurse, and had to work at Frederick Road Hospital. She must have just been in the age group to be called up, so went back to nursing and couldn't really come to see me much; she only ever came about twice. She came to my aunt's at Harpenden, and I went over there to see her. My brother used to come over occasionally, he was at St Albans but he would never come to my billet, I would meet him in Welwyn Stores, we thought it was better that way. When my father came once, they did invite him in but he stood just inside the front door and then we went out for a meal. They never fed him, I don't know what he thought about the billet really, because I seemed reasonably happy to him, I was not complaining. We didn't have to write home from that school like we did in the village but I did write, I used to enjoy writing home. I don't know that I really missed my mother very much, I think if I had not had my aunt, her younger sister, to visit I possibly would have done, but that was a saving grace.

When I came back to Hastings the war was still on, and I remember the bomb being dropped on Emmanuel Church, just nearly next door to our house, I was there. My mother was on night duty that night and my father had to go out as the air raid warning had gone and of course I was in the house alone. I was asleep, I can still hear it - that BANG. I was asleep and it woke me up. My father came back quickly after the bomb had dropped and took me to Margaret's house, her house was even nearer to where the bomb had dropped, just on the opposite pavement but they'd got an air raid shelter so we all went into that, but my parents hadn't one. They were never afraid in air raids because of their experiences in the First World War when they were nursing behind the Front Line. The vicarage and church were badly damaged and the vicar's little two-year-old daughter was killed.

Emmanuel Vicarage, hit on May 3, 1942

This picture shows the bomb damage to Emmanuel Vicarage (recorded in *Hastings & St. Leonards in the Front Line* 1985 (2<sup>nd</sup> Edition) Published by the Hastings & St. Leonard's Observer. First Edition published in 1945 by F J Parsons for the Observer.)

The war finished soon after that, but of course before that happened we had the doodlebugs coming over. They didn't really bother us too much because we knew they were aiming to go to London. The Spitfires tried to tip them into the sea as they came over. There were two Spitfires, Gert and Daisy they were called, it was quite interesting to watch them trying to tip the doodlebugs into the sea before they got to land.

I could accept that my mother was on night duty during the war and my father was working with the Civil Defence but I was nearly sixteen by then and my brother Ned didn't come home to live ever, not from being evacuated. He went to London to live with my aunt to do a course in catering at Battersea Polytechnic but he never lived at home again. He used to come home for holidays, I suppose, but I don't seem to remember us being a family unit again really. When I left school, I went to Philpotts at St Leonard's, working in the dressmaking department, which to me was fairly a waste of time because all I wanted to do was to go nursing, but you couldn't until you were older. It was a five year training in this department, I was just a junior and only there for a year. I was allowed to turn up hems and sew on buttons, so I suppose that helps, to sew on buttons. Otherwise I was the junior who made the tea and picked up pins that were on the floor. I joined the Red Cross and every Saturday I used to go to The Royal East Sussex Hospital on the Children's Ward and I really enjoyed that. I used to wash the children and feed them and that was very interesting and enjoyable and quite a good grounding for a nursing career.

I think really the war did me a lot of good, because before I went away my parents doted on me a little, and I didn't help much in the house. My mother had the Bed and Breakfast and I enjoyed serving breakfasts but otherwise did nothing. It was a very happy childhood; we used to go away for holidays and had quite a happy time before the war. But I think I benefited especially from that latter billet, being with such an intelligent man who obviously saw in me a daughter that he hadn't had. He encouraged me so much with what I wanted to do, and what I was doing; he did help me, I'm sure he matured me and helped me to speak well, not like the first billet where they all swore. He was different from them and gave me a bit of culture, which possibly I might not even have had with my own parents. They were very loving and very religious but I don't feel they had too much culture about them; although my auntie Chris had, my father's sister.

I don't think it did me any harm at all. It made me see life, I suppose, especially the first family. When I was at the second billet I was lucky to have relations near that I could visit and my brother came to see me when I was with my aunt sometimes, and all in all I think it did me quite a bit of good. I always wanted to be a nurse, it didn't change that one bit and it didn't affect my religious life, I stuck to my own ideals. Once I had gone home, I forgot about the war, although after I went nursing I did go back to see them, just once, and then when I came back from Kenya when I was thirty. Mrs Hobbs had this bit of a chip on her shoulder about having to take an evacuee and perhaps she couldn't get over that and there I was but as I say, he made it bearable, very bearable and introduced me to classical books, music and the arts. I think he helped me a great deal and so did the friendly people at the church I attended.

Ellen and her brother Ned at the age they were evacuated.

# Chapter 11. 'If you're on a charge...you can't defend yourself.'

## Ned's Story. (Brother to Ellen).

My maternal grandfather was a Factor on an Estate in Stowupland, and a horse killed him quite early on. The Factor was quite a high up person on the Estate and my mother was brought up as a young gentlewoman. They lived in a tithe House, which they lost when he died, so then they became poor and my mother, instead of leading a life of leisure, had to go and be a servant and that was a big shock to her. Then the Great War came which opened up things for many people of that generation, including my mother, who could then go nursing because there was at once a shortage of nurses. She trained in the Queen Alexandra's Nursing Reserve, which is the army set of nurses at Edmonton in North London. Then she went to Netley, which is a big military hospital just outside Southampton, where she nursed people of both nationalities, British and German. I'm not quite sure about the next move but she did go to Ireland during the Black and Tan business and then she came back to England and worked in a very posh clinic, somewhere in the Harley Street area, which was, I imagine, quite a good job.

I remember her mother as a very old lady who died just before the Second World War, but I remember my paternal grandparents much better because we went to see them every holiday. We spent Christmas with them in Engadine Street, Southfields, which is near Wimbledon tennis courts. My grandfather had been a mount cutter in the top firm in the country, if you were a wealthy person and you inherited a big house and you wanted pictures you went there. He was the foreman in charge of the workshop and although he was a manual worker it was quite a highly paid job because the people who ran it were the second generation and did not know all that much about pictures, really, so he was on the management firm as well as running the men. They had quite a tough time because Madam, as they called her, a French lady who inherited the business, didn't know much about it and she used to chase them around a bit and he used to say, you know, "Madam you cannot do that", put her right, which she did not like very much. They were religious people. When they moved into Southfields it was a massive new estate of great long roads of terraced houses and they were in with the set of people who bought a bit of a field and built St Luke's Church; they were very keen and he became a Sidesman. My mother's people were religious as well; they were very keen Methodists, so both my parents came from a very religious background.

My father worked in a Shipping Office in Southfields before the Great War and like everybody else he volunteered on the first day, but he was medically unfit and carried on working in the Shipping Office for the first two years. After the massive losses in 1916 Britain had a big re-think. Up to then the French had provided all the hospitals in France, they said, "This is our country, we can organise this," but they couldn't; so the British said, "Look, you are not doing it right," and agreed to take over. They had two sorts of hospitals, one taking battle casualties and another hospital where they dealt with the men who became ill with influenza for instance. So my father volunteered again and this time they said, "Ah yes you can come", so he joined the Royal Army Medical Corps.

They hadn't got sufficient kit in those days, so first of all they worked from home and he went to a local Drill Hall in the city, where they drilled and did all the things that the army do. Then first the puttees would come and they would wear those, then the jacket would come and they would wear that, and gradually their kit was built up. So you see, they lived at home and drilled while they assembled their kit. Then one day the Sergeant Major said, "Right I've got the travel warrant, get on this train," and they went down to Byfleet, where they went to a former racing track. It became the Army's motorised training depot and two of them were allocated an ambulance. Bear in mind that these men had only seen a car but they had never ridden in one; after some circuits on the track that was their training, they were a motorised Ambulance Column and they drove down to Dover straight on to the ship across to the other side and drove to this hospital, where they began their nursing. They would be sent round to where the local units were to pick up ill soldiers, but not up to the Front Line.

My father said he didn't deal with any battle cases, but he kept a diary and if there was a big gas attack, the main hospitals were flooded and the one where he was based had to deal with the gas casualties at times. He carried on with that until the end of the war, which ended with an armistice. Both armies had agreed that the one who got a break through first would win and on the 30th October the British Army broke through in two places, the French broke through in another and the Australians broke through, there were four 'break throughs'; the German lines were smashed. The cavalry, which they always had on hand, charged through the gaps. They rode for three miles but there was no one to kill, they had to be recalled because there weren't any Germans there; the Germans collapsed and they had to ask for an armistice. Everybody forgets that an armistice is only a temporary cessation; it's like a truce, and they agreed to have a truce for six months and then start again. The army repatriated some troops but they kept some out there, in what they called a cadre, which is like a central core of the army which would re-open possibilities in April 1919. The Germans dithered and the British and French brought up ammunition and said, "We are ready to go, if you do not sign the Versailles Treaty, we shall start the bombardment, we shall move forward again for war." The Germans collapsed of course and signed; then they didn't need the cadre any more, so my father came back and he got a job at Fraser Nash, which was a motor company.

The First World War had changed Britain completely. Until then the means of transport was mainly horses and a few cars for wealthy people but the war made this re-appraisal take place, and Britain said, "We are going to have a motorised army from now on," and people like my father could drive of course. In those days you didn't have to have a licence to drive if you could get in a car you just drove, and of course he could drive, so he went to Fraser Nash and made cars. That lasted for some time and then he went back into the Army Medical Service at Farnborough, they had some kind of wartime re-union there and he met my mother and they married. That was when they went to Hastings and he went into the removal business. They bought a big house with the idea that they would start a nursing home; it was a house of four storeys so they could live in part of it and use the rest for the business, but of course Ellen and I came along so they never did.

My father was a very keen member of the Church of England; he was Churchwarden of Emmanuel Church for twenty-five years. My mother was an equally keen Methodist. Up to 1932 there were three sorts of Methodists, and on Sunday mornings she went to Culvert Road Primitive Methodist in Hastings and in the week she went to their Women's Fellowship and on Sunday evenings she went with my father to the Anglican Church and was also a member of the Emmanuel Women's Fellowship as well. Both of them were in fact very keen and deeply religious people, and at one time my grandparents came and had a holiday in Eastbourne. My father was running this motor business and could only have Sunday off and they had a big discussion before they went on the train to see them, because it would mean they were breaking the Sabbath to go on the train and they had to think about that, but they did decide to go.

I attended church with my father quite often and I attended Sunday school and in those days you started school at three. For the first two years you were in the Junior Department, which was just playing games with these well-meaning ladies who liked children and that sort of thing. I was a very thin, skinny child and they came and grabbed you and crushed the breath out of you with their hugs; I hated it. But in the top class there was a nurse Duvall and she was the tall skinny type, just like me and she wouldn't touch you, she was actually quite 'with it'. One of the things she had us do was to learn the Benedictus, and the best one was to get a prize. Well I was determined to win and went to my father and said, "What is this Benedictus?" He showed it to me in the prayer book and I said, "Well how do you learn it?" He said, "What you do, you have the prayer book open and read the first line... Blessed be the Lord God of Israel... and then you close it and see if you can say it, and then you add the second line and go on". Well, in three weeks I could say this really well but I couldn't understand a word of it. Why does God only visit people? Why in David's house? Why not in Tom or Dick's house? What's this, 'To perform the oath which he swore to our forefather Abraham?' It was rote learning, and although I couldn't understand a word, I could say it.

There was going to be this prize giving so I went down to Mendham Hall where the Sunday school was held and as I went in through the gate, so I changed. My body temperature dropped and my brain moved forward at three times the speed it normally did, everything was happening in slow motion, I was cool, calm and collected. I didn't know that phrase then, but that's what I was. I was completely confident and I was going to do it well, and of course I did. We went through all the hymns and the messing about, then nurse Duvall got the register and we started at the top but none of the others had done it. What she was doing was saying, "Blessed be the Lord God of Israel," and then saying, "Carry on." I thought in my heightened state that seemed awfully slow but when she got to me, of course I was the last being T, there were no W's so I was the last. Poor nurse Duvall had her heart in her boots because no one had done it. So I let her say it twice and the second time I said it with her in my heightened state, and then went through and got the prize. But from then on I always knew that in a difficult situation where it mattered, my temperature would drop, my brain would move forward at this fast speed and I would become completely competent. You don't think you are going to get that out of Sunday school do you? I had learnt something else, and after that there was the Scholarship, the big thing in those days. In each of the exams I had this cool, calm and collected period; it was replayed there and I knew I would pass. I was completely confident. I went to the Grammar School, and the first year of course was in peacetime. That was good, but I noticed there were two kinds of lad in the school; there were some thugs, people who were bombastic and well built, and people like me who were not well-built and very quiet, there were the two sides to it. I was also in the Boy's Brigade and we were in camp the week before the war started and we were in a field with the tents and all that sort of thing. Two fields away there was a railway line and then of course there were these long trains of evacuees. The great thing was they were coming from Bermondsey but they had money and they threw pennies to us. I, who had hardly seen any money, got sixpence, six whole pennies. They came but they didn't settle down in Hastings and they went back.

On the 3$^{rd}$ September 1939 I was at home of course, just sitting there and I heard Chamberlain say, "I have to tell you that we have not received any word from Germany, we are therefore now at war with Germany." My father came back from church and said, "What did he say?" and my mother and I said, "It is the war" and he went back to the church and it was announced from the pulpit that we were now at war with Germany. At first nothing very much happened, it was a phoney war, when suddenly the Germans raced through France and it was clear the French were finished, and there were refugees coming through Hastings, and there were soldiers coming back in boats, and they were in a pretty poor state.

The war went from bad to worse, and clearly we were going to be evacuated and all schoolwork stopped. We read things like The Wind in the Willows and had more sport and there were no lessons. The other thing that happened was that the cane was brought back. Before the war there were detentions, which was half hour of sitting and writing, and there were punishment drills for lesser offences, ten minutes of Physical Training, but the war came and the cane came back and that carried on right up to the day we were evacuated. The day was a Sunday and we came to the school and all the masters had brassards on, with Evacuation Officer on them, which I thought was rather funny. We got on this train and it went painfully slowly, it went on for ages and ages.

Of course I was with all my class and I knew everyone in the compartments around me. We knew the evacuation was coming because the lessons had stopped, and then there was this unusual performance of more sport and keeping us amused really. The books disappeared because they were all boxed up so it wasn't a shock at all. I was in six weeks of my thirteenth birthday and although the Jews get their Bar Mitzvah right, as far as I'm concerned, obviously I was still a child at that stage. We had this long journey and we arrived eventually at St Albans. We waited on the station for ages and then buses took us to the billeting area where we were going to be allocated billets. I got cold feet at this stage and thought, "Oh dear". Ray Smith was there, a boy in my class, a chap I knew but was not particularly friendly with. He was there with his brother Donald who was two years younger. So I asked them if I could join them for a three and they said, "Yes". So when we came to the front of the queue and spoke to the billeting lady sitting at the table, we said, "We're three." And she looked round and she said, "Yes, three."

The bus took us to an Estate of new, very new houses right on the edge of St Albans; it was just an ordinary semi-detached house. These people whose name was McCullock had said they would take three. Mr McCullock was a Scot obviously with a name like that was some kind of construction worker. I don't really know what he did but he was only there at weekends and then he was away on construction sites. Mrs McCullock was a young woman with a young son, who was only a baby really. So we started there and we all slept in one bed in the big bedroom and Mr and Mrs McCullock and the baby had the other one.

The Head said that after being allocated a billet, at 6 o'clock he would see all the school in the main hall, so Ray and I went to this big meeting. The Head walked on, in his academic gown and he said, "From now on I act in loco parentis" and we realised that there was no power that he didn't have. "From now on," he said, "We shall be operating from four schools and I shall want you in the right school, with the right books at the right time. If any of these requirements are not met, I shall not argue, it's the cane straight away; summary execution will be given." We were allocated Spicer Street Congregational Church, a whacking great church with a ground floor, a large balcony and a hall with four rooms off it that would take three hundred. That was the place where the books were to be kept and you had to get all the right books and yourself to the right place and be there on time. Some lessons were to be held there at Spicer Street in the church itself and the four rooms, so there was enough room for five classes only. We were to use the Secondary Modern School for the labs and St Albans School was for our use in the afternoons, the whole school, while they went out, that was the way it was going to operate. The masters who took Greek at Hastings were two old men who were former lawyers and they decided to retire, so the school couldn't offer Greek any more but they upped science, we did science, science, science. Fortunately I liked science; I really understood chemistry and physics.

For the first week I was terribly homesick, I missed my mum; I was so upset. But during that week, when I was walking across Holywell Hill, which is the main road into St Albans, I saw my father's van with his name on the side; it was unmistakable. I thought, "There's my father's van, driving up the hill, how strange." Anyway he had got someone moving from Hastings to be with their children and when he had delivered his load, he came to me at Mrs McCullocks's and, bearing in mind that it was within five or six weeks of my birthday, he bought me a very nice bathing costume. It was royal blue and a beautiful fit and I thought it was a lovely garment and as St Albans at that time still had the use of the swimming pool and we were allowed to use it free, along I went. We had a chap named Matthews, who was in charge; I was in

Norman house and he was the games Supremo and he taught me to swim. He didn't worry if you did it wrong, he'd say, "Have another go," he was a very good teacher because he knew how difficult it was; he was not one of these natural athletes.

We didn't start school properly until the middle of September, because although the books had been crated up, they just didn't come. I'd go to the swimming pool in the morning and Matthews would give me a quarter of an hour, then after lunch he'd give me another quarter of an hour, so whereas I'd lived in Hastings all my life and had only been in St Albans a month, I'd learnt to swim well there. I could also see that I was going to be able to work this system because of getting to his classes on time and I said to myself, "This evacuation is for me," and in that month, with the swimming and turning up at the right time I got the knack of it and thought, "I can handle this". I'd got over my longing for my mother and I got on well with the two brothers Ray and Donald but we didn't get on too well with Mrs McCullock it was too much for her. She wasn't used to young boys and she got bothered because we took up most of her time and she couldn't handle it basically, so there was a bit of friction. After we'd been there about three weeks we had to transfer to another billet and she said, "From next Saturday, you will be with the Smiths," which was four doors down the road. She said, "I've talked to Mrs Smith and she said she'll take you." So that was it, we transferred from Mrs McCullock to the Smith's house.

There was Mr Smith, Mrs Smith and their son Ray Smith, so we'd got two Rays. Her son was a year older than us, he'd be thirteen, so she was used to young boys, and she was a motherly lady and treated us very well. Mr Smith's legs were as long as legs should be, but from there on he was half the size because his back was foreshortened and he'd got a big hump. He'd been brought up as an orphan and been given proper training as a tailor so he could make clothes and fit people right from the start. If you wanted a suit, he would measure you up, tack it all up, arrange a fitting and make any changes and he used to make Mrs Smith's clothes but they never wore out. He worked in Nicholson's, who manufactured raincoats in St Albans. So the best part of the morning he would work for them and then in the evening he made suits for people, with cloth he had bought. He had been trained right from cloth to finished garment. I was very happy there and felt evacuation was for me. Then school started and I got the knack of getting the books and getting to the right place. One day I was late, so of course I was given the cane. I was standing in line, another chap went forward and bent over and the master went *whack* and all of us disappeared in a cloud of dust, obviously this chap had been sliding down in the dust. The master accused him of having a book in his trousers. I got my punishment as well and then it happened fairly frequently. That was all right. I didn't mind being punished, if the Head thought he'd got to do that, then that was up to him. I didn't worry about it, it didn't affect me, I didn't think, "This is bad" or anything.

After the first six weeks of being evacuated the Head had announced, "I'm not having you people lying in bed and doing nothing on Sundays. There are four churches, you can choose one and you will go there, and a master will turn up to mark that you are present". So I went to St Steven's, which was near where I was living and attended church every Sunday morning. The only way you could get out of it was if your parents came up and you showed the Head the letter your parents had sent. The Maidstone and District Bus Company ran a bus each Sunday to St Albans for the parents, arriving about half past ten, just before the church service, so you wouldn't be able to go, they left about six o'clock. Ray and Donald's parents came up frequently but my father couldn't because of his work. At the start of the war he had two lorries for his business, one was moderately new that he'd bought in '38, that was commandeered, (taken away from him by the army) but he'd still got the older one. After the first flush of everyone wanting to leave Hastings there were no more removal jobs, so he closed his business down and joined the Air Raid Precaution service as a permanent warden, he was always on duty. He also got the job of taking the meals round for people on continuous duty. He drove around in his lorry with big thermos flask things to all the ARP posts; he couldn't leave every weekend because he was always on duty.

When I got to sixteen I had to register and go to an approved Youth movement of some kind. It could be the Scouts or it could be The St John's Ambulance or anything like that. You had to go to one and you had to register and say, "I'm going to this." One of the masters, Mr Miller, had started the Air Training Corps and I was interested in being a pilot, so that was for me. Bare in mind I was pretty unfit really. I went and saw him and said, "I'm not that fit, you know, but could I join?" And he said, "Oh yes, dead keen." So that was a good move because we met twice a week. One night it was PT, marching and the other techniques of flying. It meant you couldn't do homework on those nights, so it was given early and you were given class time to do your homework and that went on until we took the School Certificate. One good thing that happened was when I was taking the General Schools Certificate in '44, it was just before D Day and the army were having big manoeuvres. The exam was held in one of the classrooms at the top of St Stephen's Hill, and we were having this French Oral exam for half an hour just at the moment when the tanks of the attacking force were wanted. These tanks were in low gear, driving up St Stephen's Hill, their tracks were slipping on the road, steel on concrete, so you can just imagine how very noisy it was, the examiners couldn't hear a word. The convoy of tanks were flat out and they were roaring away, so the exam had to stop and it had to be written in about the tanks and everybody was told they would pass. They had to do that because we just couldn't be heard, so the war had its advantages because everybody passed the French Oral.

Another thing on offer but not compulsory was that you could attend St. Albans Cathedral and be prepared by Bishop's Chaplain, who was a marvellous young man, for Communion by Confirmation. I took advantage of that and my mother did come up when I was confirmed and made quite a thing of it. I was about fifteen or sixteen by that time but there was one very young lad who also wanted to be confirmed. Someone had to make sure he did the right thing at the right time, so I was given charge of him and didn't have time to be nervous because I was worrying what he was doing, so that was a good thing. I was confirmed by Bishop Bell of Chichester in St Albans Abbey because we were still under his jurisdiction

My parents were very phlegmatic about the bombing in Hastings. The Germans did come over at times but they didn't get up; they didn't go to the shelter or anything, they would just turn over and go to sleep and strangely enough I found I did the same thing. St Albans was interesting really, for a safe area. One particular night a plane that was obviously low down had dropped its bombs right across the estate where I was living. I woke up and heard wee... ee... ; there were six bombs, a stick. I just woke up and heard the noise and thought, "Oh yes," and went back to sleep again. And I was surprised, going to school next day to find that most people had got up and made tea and dressed and stayed up for the rest of the night. That day my friends and I were out there on the estate looking and we found an unexploded bomb, the crater was only about a foot across, just a puddle really. The area round the estate was very marshy and the bomb had just gone into the ground and not exploded but we didn't find any shrapnel or anything, nothing of interest. The other thing was that a searchlight battery was placed in a field near us and at night the searchlights were lit and they moved over the sky and flashed around but they never picked up anything; they were a complete waste of time really, but looked good and it was quite close, and we liked talking to the people there. We were all issued with gas masks, which we had to wear and mine got awfully bashed around because I didn't allow for it when I was going round corners.

All this time I never went home, no, I never went home, but I went to see my sister; sometimes I went to Welwyn Garden City. As the war went on the Second Front opened and it quietened down as far as England was concerned, and evacuees were allowed to go back to Hastings if they wished, and the schools reopened. Ray and Donald's parents had visited regularly every fortnight and they were homesick, and as soon as it was possible they badgered their parents to take them back and they did. They left, I think, shortly after the opening of the Second Front, these two friends I'd lived with all the time. But I'd set myself up for this earlier on, anticipating it. I noticed that at the end of the evacuation the 'thuggish boys', the toughies that were really the mother's boys, had gone home. It was the not so robust, quiet types that were left, very noticeable, but that was the way it was at the end, it was something about the boys themselves. Outwardly those who were tough, physically strong and muscular weren't as tough as they looked, and the outwardly weaker ones, in my opinion were the strong ones.

The war was coming to an end and the last thing that happened for me was at the Air Training Corps when Mr Miller who ran it took us to camp. We went to Harwell, which nowadays is the Atomic Research Station. It was a heavy bomber base then, and it was fun for the first two or three days. The bombers were being got ready for action and the crews were pleased to see us in the Lancasters and they showed us how the controls worked and how it all happened. Mr Miller said we could have a flight provided our parents gave us permission. I thought, "That's a bit much isn't it, to write to your parents and say 'please give me permission to fly in an aircraft and I may be killed'. What parents give that sort of permission?" So I didn't write. But when it came to the selection for the first flights on the Thursday the Sergeant selected me so off I went. First of all we had to go and get a parachute, you couldn't have a flight without a parachute. We got in the Jeep and we went to the Lancaster and there it was with the engines roaring, then they said, "Right, ready?" and we got on board, but then something wasn't right and they had to strip the engine out again, so we were sitting waiting there. During this time Mr Miller found that I had been sent, so a Jeep came tearing up and I was pulled off and I was court marshalled for not having my parents' consent, this was a serious offence. There was Mr Miller and two other officers and you know the paraphernalia that the military likes and they told me what a rotter I was. That put me right off the Air Force. I thought, "If that's the way they treat people, that's it!" Also the crew had had a bombing raid that night and half the bombers didn't come back. Everybody had known the young chaps who were the life and soul of the party and they were no longer there. The place was like a morgue; it was terrible. We went round the camp and they didn't want to know us of course, it was terrible and I thought, "The Air Force has had it as far as I'm concerned." I didn't explain to the officers my philosophy about not writing to my parents, I kept that to myself. It was clear to me there was nothing to be said so I didn't say anything. The way the military operates, that's the way it is, there is no excuse. I was used to the Head's system of punishment, of course, and that's the way the military operates, there are no excuses. If you're on a charge, that's it; you're guilty; you can't defend yourself.

My mother's philosophy was the one for me. When I was a younger child of five, six or seven and she had bathed me and was drying me with a towel, she would just stop and look at me sometimes and say, "Do you know, you have been born with a silver spoon in your mouth?" I would laugh and open my mouth and say, "There's only teeth and tongue in there, no spoon." And she would say, "Ah, ah, ah" and that ah, ah, ah meant titter you may, but I know that I am right and strangely enough she was, so that sort of philosophy more than the oppressive one has predominated for me. I had been looking forward to joining the Air Force, so then it was a question of what to do. I had no idea, but I had read about psychology and there was this set up in London on the issue of career psychology, where you could go and be assessed, so I talked my parents into that. My mother came with me and we went to this place where they did a test and decided I was suitable to train as a chef. They suggested the Westminster Training Institute as the best in the country, and of course it was. It was near where my aunt had lived with my grandparents at Southfields, they had died during the war so she had room for me to board with her. That meant I didn't have to go back to Hastings with my parents, which was great, I didn't want to go back.

The general effect of evacuation for me was right. I was within six weeks of my thirteenth birthday, ready to become a man, ready to take charge. Once I had taken charge as an independent person, I didn't want to go back to my parents again and in fact I never did. Obviously at the end of my military service I went for a couple of months and at odd times between things, but I never really went back home. I liked to be independent I could handle it. My feelings about going back home were that it would make me dependent again, they could have said, "Do this, do that" couldn't they?" whereas I was much more independent and wanted to be free of dependence.

For me evacuation was good, I was just ready for it, but I did get cold feet in the billeting room. I wasn't completely isolated though, nor was I completely independent. Living with my aunt I became the son she never had and she was a bit of a mother to me. In fact I looked after her all the rest of her life. Nephews I've found with single aunts often come in when they are hospitalised. They are the ones that step in and do the things that have to be done, and we were fond of each other.

So the main effect for me was that evacuation helped me to grow up quickly. It was a shock, it did give me a shock, but yes, I was ready for it. Once I found that I could operate correctly and be at the right place or school at the right time with the right books generally I was all right. The Headmaster's dictates suited me, I never worried about the punishment he dished out or the court martial, I didn't worry about that either, I didn't feel it was unjust. I never offered any excuses, because the Head would not have listened and there could have been none to Mr Miller, could there, I had gone to this aircraft without permission.

My friends and my foster parents were not religious, it didn't enter their lives at all; but we had to go to church right through the years we were evacuated. The Head kept that up all the time, which was all right for me. Of course St Stephen's was very like Emmanuel the church at home, and it was well attended by lots of prosperous men. It was a small church building and when the choir did a descant all these men would grind away and flatten the choir with their marvellous heavy bass voices coming in, it was wonderful. The school provided everything social wise, it was open during the holidays so that you could play games or run on the tracks. I was evacuated for about four years and very happy with the boys I was billeted with, but we didn't keep in touch, I can't even remember saying goodbye. I didn't visit my foster parents again but I saw the house was still there when I visited the cathedral. Apart from that first bombing raid St Albans wasn't bombed, but we didn't feel safe there because we could see London burning.

## Chapter 12

### Margaret's Story.

My name is Margaret; I was born in 1931. My parents were married in 1925 and I had a brother who was born in 1926, John, and a brother who was born in 1927 but unfortunately did not live. Even as a small child, when I was big enough to think how things were, I realised that my mother never really wanted a little girl, she only wanted another boy. Looking back, I now understand that she was never allowed to grieve for this baby, the one she had lost, so when I was born in 1931 my father seemed disappointed, which I can't remember, obviously, but even as a small child I realised that I was very much second best. My mother did not want any more children anyway but when she found she was going to have another one, she had to put up with it, as people did in those days. So some of my memories, particularly of the early days are very much of being a child who wasn't particularly wanted by her mother, but my father always tried to make it up to me.

The idea of the First War was always very much in our house, because my father had been wounded. He was deafened as a result of a battle that he was in and also he had a bullet in his right arm, and it affected the use of it. The biggest effect it had on him, which made him very bitter for the rest of his life (and he lived to be eighty-five), was the fact that he couldn't ever get a permanent job. There were no concessions made for ex-service men in those days. In the 30s there was a lot of unemployment and he worked in the Post Office as a temporary Postman, but he couldn't be made permanent because he couldn't pass the medical due to his war injuries, and this was always a big bone of contention to him. So I was brought up always knowing the effects of war. He didn't talk about the battle he was in; he was at the Somme, I think, but he did talk about what happened to him later in the First World War. He worked in Woolwich Arsenal, filling shells in the danger area and because of the explosive his hair went white. In fact when I can first remember him it was almost yellow because of the effect of the Cordite, one of the constituents of the explosive.

In 1939, and before that when there was talk of war, I can remember Mr Chamberlain coming back from Munich in 1938 and waving a bit of paper. I'm not quite sure how we knew he waved a bit of paper because there was no television. We had a radio, a wireless it was called in those days. We listened to that and I can remember hearing about it, and by then I could read and I used to read the papers. If there was anything of particular interest my mother was a great one for cutting out pictures and cuttings from the papers, so they would be around the house. I remember Sunday the 3rd of September 1939. I was sitting on the front steps of where we were living in Hollington and I could hear the broadcast by the Prime Minister from the living room in the house, and not long afterwards the siren went. Of course we'd all been told what the siren was, we'd all got gas masks. I remember going indoors and saying to my mum, "Do I need my gas mask?" Soon after that the All Clear went, it was obviously a false alarm, a British plane or something, so that's the first thing I remember about the war.

At the same time or just after that; I don't think they came until the war started; we had three little boys who were evacuated from the East End of London billeted with us. Two of them were brothers and there was another, a little boy called Derek. We were not a well-off family, although my mother came from quite well off farming people; my grandmother had a farm outside Battle. My father's family had been builders at Westerham and had built a lot of property, particularly a lot of chapels. My grandfather built the one at Tenterden and others all through the Weald of Kent. But because my father had never been able to get a very good job because of his war injuries we didn't have very much money; what money we did have he preferred to save rather than spend; he'd always got money, but unfortunately he didn't choose to spend it. So we weren't very well off, but these children who came from London obviously had been very poor. I don't think they had very much in the way of clothes before they came but they had been given a jumper and trousers, boots and an overcoat, they'd been issued with those to come away in.

Derek came from a home where there were older brothers and I think they were perhaps a little better off than the other family of Wilfred and Billy (the brothers), because they had, I think, ten children in that family; but Derek was the naughty boy. I remember him becoming very fond of my mother and as she always preferred boys of course she made a fuss of those three evacuees, as she always did my brother, and I probably felt even more left out than before. Derek really didn't know what was his own; he was very naughty. He stole from one or two shops and my mother would have to go down and try and sort it out because he came home with things he shouldn't have, and he would also steal things from the school. One day he came home with these packets of needles, which for some reason my mother never took back - I don't know why - but for years after that there were these half to a dozen packets of sewing needles and she'd even got them when she died; this was when she was eighty-five, so it was a lot of years later. Wilfred and Billy's mother came down to see them once with two or three more children. They stayed until getting on towards Christmas and then they all went back because it was the time of the 'phoney war'. There was nothing much going on and they thought they'd be just as well at home in London. So my first experience of evacuation was the ones that lived with us.

We come around now to July 1940 when I remember my father coming home and saying that he'd heard we had to be evacuated, and it was compulsory and all the children had to go. There were quite a number of people getting together in little knots, groups of people saying, "Well I'm not letting my children go, they're not going". "Well if it's compulsory you'll have to let them go". It was then realised it wasn't compulsory, it was a voluntary thing, but it was decided that we would go. My brother was fourteen and at Silverhill School. I had to go with him because younger children went with older brothers and sisters but strangely enough, the school I went to was also in the Silverhill area. It was a small church school called St Matthews, which was also evacuated to London Colney, so I went to the same place as my brother.

It's quite near St Albans, just outside, about four miles. I remember the train journey very well the day we went; it was a steam train. Part of the time I stood in the corridor with one of the male staff from the school, a man who was smoking his pipe. I was nine and I stood in the corridor with him. I don't think I was frightened; I was a self-possessed child. I just think it had been so instilled in us that there was a war on, and because there was a war on you had to do everything you were told, and it seems a very strange thing to say, but I think I was probably a very obedient child. You wouldn't have had my parents and not been obedient. I mean I found out that it was much easier to do what you were told than kick against the traces because you soon got into trouble. They never punished me but my father used to 'strap' my brother, he was really treated quite badly by my father, but not my mother. This was a very strange thing but my father always made a fuss of me, he spoilt me a lot but my mother never did.

I was expected to be quite grown up from an early age; in those days children were sent to the shop and that sort of thing. We lived in Old Church Road, Hollington and it was quite a long way down to Battle Road, but I was often sent to the shops from probably four or five onwards; nobody thought anything about it in those days; you went with a note and the money wrapped up in the note in your hand tight, so you didn't lose it. I often went to the shops like that; if it wasn't the day the butcher's boy called for orders I was sent to the shop. The other thing is I went to school when I was three. I've still got the letter that the Headmistress wrote to say she would take me into the school, that was in the August following my third birthday in May, so I think I was probably a self-possessed little girl; but looking back now I may also have been quite a horrid child.

I didn't feel very much afraid but once I got to London Colney I was taken with a friend at the same school to a billet where I had a sense of 'I don't like this.' I was separated from my brother, the idea was that you went with your brother or sister if you had one, but he didn't want me with him. If you were fourteen and a boy you wouldn't really want a nine-year-old sister would you? The 'so called' protection didn't even last for the train journey to be quite honest; it was a myth wasn't it? We'd never been particularly close; with five years between us, as brother and sister; I can't remember us ever being very close. So I was billeted with another girl who lived a little way away from us in Silverhill; we had moved from Hollington to Silverhill just after the war started. She was heart-broken; she was very tearful, she cried, I kept saying to her, "Look, don't cry, it won't be as bad as that and you'll be all right". She was a year older than me but I was trying to look after her, that was Betty.

We were taken to this billet and there was a man, who I remember as being very dark, dark hair, very dark eyes and a big moustache, he didn't have a beard but he had this big moustache and he was not at all welcoming. His wife was Portuguese; she did speak English but not terribly well. He worked at Hill End Psychiatric Hospital, I don't think he was a trained nurse, but he was what they called in those days an attendant. As soon as I went into the house I can remember feeling a very strange atmosphere. He totally dominated his wife who had come over to work as a domestic in the hospital and then they got married. They had one little girl, who was three years old, called Marie. Obviously looking back, I didn't realise it at the time because you don't, she resented us going into the home. I've still got the mark where she forced a knitting needle into my leg so she obviously made it very plain and I just felt that her parents wanted us, one for our rations and two for the money they got for us. It was ten shillings and sixpence and eight shillings for the second evacuee if you were unaccompanied and I just felt they wanted us for the money.

I suppose I was a bit cheeky - I certainly wasn't a child to keep quiet; I'd say my piece. Although I had to behave myself at home, I wasn't in any way suppressed; I'd always been allowed to say things. No one had ever grumbled at me for saying things, it was just as long as you didn't do anything you were told not to do.

We weren't given any butter and we should have had two ounces but we had just a horrible sort of spread that was like lard; it was really horrible and I hated it. We'd always had good food at home, we weren't very well off but we'd always had excellent food so I hated it and I wanted my butter. I remember saying to her one day, "Why don't we have our butter?" and she said, "I need that". I can't remember her accent but what she meant was she needed it for Marie, because Marie was a baby and Marie had to have it. I never had any eggs all the time I was there either; I never had an egg. She kept them for Marie; and the man, he was really horrible, he didn't hit us but he would hold on to your arm tight. If you were doing anything that he didn't think you ought to be, he would hold on to your arm, really, really tight. I can remember him doing that lots and lots of times; I didn't like it. The other thing this man did, he used to look after my pocket money and I never got back the amount I should have had. I didn't have much, six pence a week or something but I know there was a discrepancy about how much money there was supposed to be. The other girl's mother came shortly because she was so unhappy and decided they would all be evacuated, so she came and collected her and they went off to Somerset. So I was left there on my own.

By October my father had gone to Hayes to work in aviation and he came to see me and he picked up that I wasn't happy, but I wouldn't have told him very much - you didn't. Then as things got worse at home my mother was evacuated. The situation did get much worse and they really thought there was going to be an invasion so she was evacuated with a friend of ours, my Godmother. My mum came to London Colney and lived there for a few weeks; not very far away from where I was, about ten minutes walk and she also realised that things were not as they should be and she found me another place, which was very nice. My mother didn't live with me, she lived up the road with the local Funeral Director. I did see her but she was only there for a short while, for a few weeks and then she went home, but I stayed there. Again I was expected to be very adult in this billet. They were very nice people with two children, Violet and Roy who were both younger than me but although they were very, very, kind, very nice people, they still expected me to be quite grown up. Every Saturday I was sent on the 84 Bus, usually I took Violet with me and we had to go and stand in the queue at Jo Lyons teashop because they had cakes which weren't rationed but in very short supply, so you had to go about eight in the morning and you queued until the shop opened for whatever they had. Maybe you got a Swiss Roll, maybe you got a few Bath Buns, what there was you had, and then I had to get the bus and go back. It was quite an expedition and then I was always sent to buy my foster mother's sanitary towels when I was still only nine or ten, so I did quite a lot of shopping and all that sort of thing. But they were very nice people, they were warm and happy and generous. I got on very well and stayed there until I left London Colney in 1942, when I went to the High School.

The strange thing about it was that I used to come home for holidays, my teacher lived near us in Silverhill and she had a car and would save her petrol so she could go home for holidays, and she used to take me with her. In a way I suppose it was a bit like boarding school and going back home for holidays. But there was bombing here in Hastings and on one occasion I went up to Hollington to see a friend. We walked down to the Church in the Wood and a German plane came over. They used to come over and start shooting bullets all over the place, they called it strafing, machine gunning. We were walking down the road to the hall of the Church in the Wood as this plane came over. We dived into a ditch and the bullets were flying all around us but then we got up and walked on. And now when I think about it, I think, "Why did we?" But then again I know it was because the war was on. There were people killed that I knew. There was quite severe bombing at Silverhill and one of the friends I was evacuated with, her mother was killed and the baby she had just had died in that bombing at Silverhill. I could see the sense of evacuation and yet you could just as well have been killed when you came home, to come home for holidays did seem a bit strange.

London Colney was quite near to London and we used to hear the blitz and see all the lights and that sort of thing. I don't remember there being any bombs in the area of London Colney itself, so of course I stayed there and took the exam for the local High School. I could have gone to St Albans High School when I passed the eleven-plus but my mother wanted me to come back home and be re-evacuated so that I could go to the Hastings High School. I came back home for the summer holidays and then met up at the end with these other girls who had passed the scholarship. There we were with our velour hats and our hatbands on, I was in Cavell House with a red hatband. We all met up at Hastings station and were put on the train yet again and taken to Ware, my mum wanted me to do that. I wouldn't have minded going to St Albans because I knew two girls that went there and I would quite liked to have gone with them, but there was no question of it.

The first thing I remember about Ware was seeing this very large lady with a big bosom on Ware station and thinking, "I hope I'm not going to live with her because I don't like the look of her very much," and that was Miss Commin the Headmistress. She'd come to meet the new girls, you see, with Paddy's mother because she was the Billeting Officer. We were all taken I believe to the Congregational Church Hall, either that or The Institute; it gets a bit vague there. I wasn't taken with a girl from the third form I was in but with a girl from the fourth called Miriam, so she was a year older than me and that meant a lot. She was a well developed girl and I was skinny and I always remember the first time I saw her get undressed, she wore a brassiere as they called them in those days, I can remember thinking how funny it was, and we just tolerated each other but we didn't do very much together. I soon found new friends from my own form as it were, and so that's how I came to be at Ware in a good billet. The lady there was interesting and the man was interesting too. He worked in a factory and she had been housekeeper to the people at Hatfield Place, - the Salisbury's, to Lord Salisbury. She had a very nice house and she was an excellent cook; we had lovely, lovely food. Although it was still rationed, it was how she managed it, I remember thinking as a child how beautiful it was because we had everything.

The man there was pro-Russia; I don't know whether he was a Communist or not but very pro-Russia. We were always hearing how wonderful the Russians were in the war and everything. They had a front room that you never went into. I'd always wanted to play the piano and they had a lovely piano, - well it seemed beautiful to me, it was beautifully polished and I longed to be able to go in and play on the keys but you weren't allowed to. I think I looked in the door once or twice and knew what was in there, but it was the front parlour and it just wasn't used. The rest of the house was comfortable, our bedroom and that, but after a bit the other girl came home, she'd got fed up with it and she came back to Hastings. Then the lady's sister was ill, so she had to go and look after her and her child. I don't quite know what the problem was, but I had to leave there, so this time I went and found my own billet.

I'd become very grown up, very worldly-wise. This next one was with a couple that hadn't got any children. He worked for Allen and Hamburys, so he was exempt from military service and she wasn't a very fit lady, rather frail but very nice. I remember saying to the Billeting Officer that I'd found my own billet and I'd be perfectly all right. I expect she thought I was a precocious kid but I stayed there until the Tuition classes started properly at home and more or less everybody came back.

We all came back and went up to the old High School. The war was still going on and the evacuation hadn't officially ended. Most people had drifted home and then Miss Commin and all the staff came home as well. I think they called it Tuition classes at the High School. I don't think they were allowed to say it was the High School although they went back to the school building. At this stage it was early '44. I think perhaps we came home for Christmas and never went back. We were home all during the buzz bombs, the doodlebugs. One landed in Pine Avenue when we were having lunch at school; we all dived under the table and the windows all came in.

I think I was probably quite pleased to come home; then I was evacuated yet again, towards the end of the war. There were the doodlebugs and then there were the V2's, the rockets. My mother had a sort of nervous breakdown, I suppose, and it was decided she should go away for a while, and so she went to Yorkshire and I went with her to Swaledale, where I went to Richmond High School for a term. We lived with the people she had been housekeeper to before she got married, a family of people who came from Battle and remembered Hastings.

So I was evacuated yet again but that was a private evacuation, it wasn't anything to do with anybody else; I think it was because my mother wasn't well. That was all right but I missed out on the High School for that one term, then I came back and went to the High School again. Well of course I was a lot further advanced educationally when I came back than when I went because the education in Yorkshire was excellent. It was a model school, they had been very settled and had no problems during the war. The school building in those days was in the architecture books, built about 1938-39, Richmond High School for girls. Although they'd had no problems and I quite enjoyed it there I still felt I wasn't very well accepted. I mean you weren't accepted, as an evacuee you'd be very much an outsider. I was good at netball and given a place in the netball team and that didn't go down very well at all because I was taking someone else's place, there was always a fuss about something. We weren't allowed to wear our outdoor shoes in school, we had to wear house shoes. There was some mud on mine one day when I had to go to the Headmistress for something and she said, "How did you get that mud on there?" And I said, "When we went to the air raid shelter". She said, "You don't miss much in life, do you dear." That's me.

I don't think the girls at Ware Grammar School accepted us either, even by the time we left. You'd have thought they'd have got used to it by the time we went, but I don't think they did. I felt very much we were intruding upon them although we didn't have many lessons at Ware Grammar School itself, but we did use their facilities. We were there in the afternoons but in the mornings we went to the Congregational Church Hall or the Institute. I always felt we were a nuisance and they felt they were a bit sort of superior to us; we were those wretched evacuees, I think it was a bit like that. At London Colney there were so few of us in a temporary building I don't think I felt very much like an outsider at all because I had quite reasonable attention, there were perhaps fifteen of us in a small class with one or two teachers, it was quite small.
When we eventually came home from Yorkshire my mum was never very well; she went on being unwell for a long time. I used to be kept home and Fanny Commin, the Headmistress used to write her letters and say couldn't she have a Home Help instead of keeping me off school to look after her. I think she was going through a very difficult 'change of life' and also she'd had a pretty tough time and it wasn't a happy marriage and I think that makes a lot of difference.

It was a bit difficult to integrate as a family again after the war because my mother had an elderly uncle. He was the local Bookmaker, and he used to have a Turf Accountant office in Whitefriars Road; he had been a farmer but he'd given that up. He came to live with us and he really was not a nice man at all, I disliked him intensely and I couldn't bear him being there, he didn't know how to treat little girls and he treated little girls in a way he shouldn't have treated little girls. Well, I suppose now they would call it child abuse; I don't think there is any other word for it but I don't think it was called that at the time. He would touch me, and my mother expected me to sleep in the same room as him.

I couldn't object, could I, because you see the house was always full. There were always people staying with us; my mother was one of those who collected up extra people because the war was on and they hadn't anywhere else to go, which is why he was there, and why several other people were there as well. I was just expected to put up with it, it was a bit risky, but then they didn't think things like that in those days did they? They didn't know those things and probably didn't take any notice but I did and when he actually went I was twelve or thirteen. I don't know why I did it; it was stupid it was a funny thing to do, but I can remember when he walked out of the door I went and washed my hands and said, "Thank God he's gone, thank heaven he's gone," because I felt glad to be rid of him.

These things happened perhaps because of the war, I don't know if they would have happened if we hadn't had a war. Well, people were all thrown together, and I think this is one of the biggest things that happened, I'm sure it didn't just happen in our family. I'm sure it happened in lots of other families, in lots of other places where people got pushed together. You were told whatever was going on, "There's a war on". I got fed up with that phrase; it was an excuse for anything; whatever happened, "There's a war on, don't you know there's a war on?" that's what they told little children all the time; this is what was said; it wasn't just parents that said it but it was everybody, it was all coming across, there was a lot of propaganda. The war changed people's morals and everything; it didn't matter what happened, there was a war on and so you had to put up with things.

My father was still away, he stayed away for two or three years after the war working for Fairy Aviation, a company that made aeroplanes and my brother was still in the Air Force, came home when they could and we just had to make the best of it really. You weren't expected to complain about anything. I had whatever there was in the way of food and clothes but when I first went to the High School I was feeling quite mortified because they used to wear three pleat gymslips and I did not have the regulation one. Someone had given my mother an old one and my Godmother who was a dressmaker turned it so mine had a different pattern to everyone else and it probably was remarked on. I had the regulation square necked blouses from Lewis Highlands; I did have three of those but that was what it was like, because I had those I should be thankful that I'd got them. Not long after that they changed to pinafore style gymslips, it was a bit strange really. There were lots of things like that but I don't know how it affected me, and I don't know how it affects me still, but I think I grew up fast, very fast. I think I learnt to make decisions for myself and became quite independent. That became quite positive and I think we probably became much more able than children of that age normally are today, we had our own opinions about things and perhaps met things you wouldn't have met up with in other circumstances, for instance you did come to realise that people were being killed.

There was so much going on and so much devastation, I'm very much a pacifist and I think it comes from this. My husband wouldn't agree but I don't think there is any justification ever for war, the horrors of war, definitely not. My husband believes in fighting for a just cause, but I find it very difficult to come to just causes for war. There are always innocent people who are hurt, and I had very much this feeling as a child, "Why should these innocent people be being killed?" We knew one child who was killed in the bombing, and why was he killed? Why should that be? It didn't make a great deal of sense. I think too you picked up a lot from people like the man I lived with who might well have been a Communist. I picked up a lot of political ideas from people. We've got three children but I don't know about their ideologies; one takes more after his father's way of thinking and although my daughter is brain damaged she's still got lots of ideas about things.

Margaret at home with her parents during one of her holidays.

## Chapter 13. 'As far as I'm concerned a lot of good came out of it.'

## Terry's Story.

**Terry in Manor Road Hastings in 1938**

I'm Terry Breeds; it was the 21$^{st}$ July 1940 when we were evacuated; there was a bit of a build up to it for several weeks beforehand when we thought we were going and then we thought we weren't. I can't remember the actual time when I was told that I was going to go away from Hastings, but I remember going, I was twelve. I went away with Mount Pleasant primary school to Walkern. I came from a widowed mother, my father died when I was two years and ten months. That would have been in 1931; I vaguely remember somebody holding me back on a little tricycle with a walking stick, that's as far as my father goes. My mother worked to bring me up on just a widow's pension, and did that by getting a few odd jobs here and there, getting a bit of cleaning work and so on and so forth.

I was singing in the choir at Emmanuel church when war was announced at eleven-o'clock in the middle of the service and the siren went. We were all getting prepared thinking we were going to get an air raid immediately, a lot people like my grandparents thinking it was like the beginning or the end of the First World War.

I can't remember how long it was before I knew I was going to be evacuated. The funny thing about it was really that my cousin, who was living in London, had previously been evacuated to Hastings. Then they suddenly realized, I think, that Hastings was in the front line if there was an invasion by sea. So not only were the people who were evacuated to Hastings sent back again, but those that were in Hastings were sent away. My cousin went to an aunt of mine at St Leonard's, very bad management.

This is what happened to us. We turned up at school and were put on trains and away we went. I felt that I was breaking with everything I knew and it was going to be a completely new experience, I just didn't know what to expect. We all had our little nametags tacked on us, I was a bit apprehensive but not frightened. When we got there to Walkern, which is a lovely little village; I can remember it very, very plainly - when we got to the school hall we were selected. A lady came to select us... you know, "I'd like this one and that one" it was almost like a cattle market I suppose, but four of us were picked out to go with this particular lady. I felt very, very, privileged, when I found out where I was going.

It felt strange, strange at first. I wondered, "Why me? Why hasn't somebody else picked me?" I was feeling a bit down to be perfectly honest. As soon as we went I was a bit wary because we'd been picked, can I say, by the lord and lady of the village. They had an old rectory on the river Lea. He was an ex-army major, retired, and they had a son and daughter themselves who were both evacuated, somebody in their own family had taken them on in Canada, and they were quite keen to do their bit by helping someone else.

So we lived in this big house and had servants waiting on us. The boys I went with were in my form, I can only think of one of them by name, but I can't think who the other two were. We shared two in a room and passed the time shooting water rats with bows and arrows that we got from the gymnasium. That was great fun.

My mother didn't want me to go, - of course not - but she felt it was better for me to go. After we'd been away for about two or three weeks, the Maidstone & District Omnibus Company put on a service for all the mums and dads to come up and see their children. Mum came and I think she was quite shocked when she found that I was living in luxury and didn't want to go back home. I'd got an uncle, her younger brother who was lodging with us, and when she got home again he said, "Well, where is he?" She was quite upset that I had turned round and said, "No, I'm happy here," when she thought I was going to go home after only a few weeks; she really thought that I'd want to go home, but I didn't.

We shared the village school building; which was great. What had happened was that Mount Pleasant School had been split up into various classes; it wasn't the whole school that was at Walkern. Part of the school was in one village and part of the school in another village and part somewhere else. We weren't integrated with the village children we had our own class with our own teacher. I lost my front teeth at Walkern, not in a fight but because I was too busy watching aeroplanes whilst there was a bit of a 'dog fight' going on overhead, when we were playing cricket out in the school field. A couple of the planes jettisoned their bombs during the cricket match as I was playing in a 'silly' something or other position, I looked up at the planes just as somebody hit the ball and it went straight into my face. When I came round in the shelter, where everyone had been taken, my front teeth were missing. The bombs were dropping around, they were only jettisoning them, but it wasn't a very safe place to be evacuated to just then, not really. I can laugh about it now, but I guess it was very scary at the time; I've still got a bit of a scar from that original experience.

Then I moved to St Albans. I'd taken the scholarship by then, the equivalent of the Eleven Plus. We found out that some of us had passed

and that we were going to the Grammar School and I can honestly say that I felt sorry that I'd got to leave there. In October, about a dozen of us moved from Walkern to St Albans, where two of us finished up being billeted together again and when we got there it was like going from the 'sublime' to the 'Gor' blimey' as we finished up in a very, very down to earth billet, a little bit more than down to earth place actually. I can't remember going to St Albans or how I got there on the journey but I can remember saying goodbye to the Major and his wife, and that was almost heart breaking, believe it or not. I wrote and was sending Christmas cards to them for years and years, even into the 1950's I was still sending cards. They were a lovely couple; loving sort of people and strangely enough I still think of those people even now. I was only there from the June to the October but I can say honestly and truthfully they played an extremely big part in my life. I learnt a lot how the 'other half' live. The very first time we went in and the table was laid I'd never seen so many spoons and forks, it was the first time I'd realised there was anything else but a knife, fork and spoon. It was a different way of life, a completely new revelation completely, completely, it was lovely.

When I transferred to St Albans from Walkern it was a different kettle of fish there. I was in that billet for several months I suppose, they had a family; there were quite a few of them there. It was, how can I say? I don't want to be demeaning or anything but it was a rather run down council property to go to from what we'd been in before - a stately English home, a very great stately home almost, you know, where there was everything you wanted, it was hard to go from that to this. I don't know what work my foster father did, I haven't a clue. They had their own children, most of them grown up; they weren't unkind, just poor, right at the other end of the scale to the Major and his wife.

Then we went to another house in St Albans and that was an extremely nice place. I don't know why we were moved to another family because neither of us asked to leave, I think for some reason they just didn't particularly want evacuees. I don't know why, I mean we weren't horrible kids in any way; we just kept ourselves much to ourselves but I really don't know why they didn't want us.

The next billet was with a dental technician in a nice area in a pre-war end of terrace house. It was a very, very nice little place and they were a nice couple. There were always false teeth on the windowsills outside because my foster father made casts of people's teeth and put them out there in the back garden. Our foster mother was a music teacher, although she wasn't really practising her trade at the time, but one day the two of us who were billeted there went up the steps together and inside the front door and heard the house resounding to the Warsaw Concerto. We stayed there for I suppose eighteen months, or something like that, and then we had to leave this one because unfortunately; well, I suppose fortunately for her, she became pregnant and with a family coming along obviously it was an encumbrance on her having two young lads around. So we moved on again.

This was the fourth 'digs', this time to a youngish mum. She'd got a young daughter and her husband was in the Services. Two of us went to her, this young mum. I suppose her child was about threeish, something like that, three or fourish, and to be honest we had some high-jinx, it was fun because she was quite young herself. There was another fellow there who had started off as an evacuee, and then he stayed on and became a lodger because when he left the London Poly he went to work down there at the Post Office as a telephone engineer, and stayed on with her as a lodger. Her husband was in the army and she'd got left with the young child; the lodger and the two of us as evacuees, so we all had to get stuck in and help her, but we had a bit of a laugh there.

This lodger taught us 'back slang,' you know when nobody knows what you're talking about. The 'back slang' consisted of an AG in front of every vowel like; it was 'lagike thagis'; 'like this', so you can talk to people and somebody else doesn't know what you're saying. We used to have a bit of a laugh with the lady there because she didn't know what we were saying and she replied, it was a bit of a laugh that was all; that was the kind of atmosphere that was there. I don't know what happened then, but we were there for some time.

At St Albans we used to use St Albans Grammar School, which was part of the old Abbey, and that in itself was an experience. I found it was a lovely, wonderful feeling, I mean to be in that building. We used to have the old basement of the building at the corner of Spicer Street and what must have been a disused school in Spicer Street. There was a girls' school at the Limes from Hastings that went back a few months before we did, and we were then able to vacate Spicer Street premises and use the Limes where the girls had been; it was a big private house, which was a good experience.

When we went up to the Grammar School from Walkern the school experience was awe inspiring, we didn't know if we were going to fit in. It was an entirely different, entirely different situation. I remember going in there and the great big quadrangle... oh my goodness! Yeah, it was a bit scary but we soon got used to it though, when we got used to it then it was good fun.

The Grammar School had very strict punishment, oh yeah! I didn't disagree with it but I remember Peter; it was a standing joke I think he was up at the Headmaster's office in the Tower practically every day of the week. The Tower was over the road joining the Abbey virtually with the school. The Headmaster's office was up in the Tower and Peter was up there getting six of the best. He was caned on the backside, yeah it was natural, it was the accepted thing, it was the normal. I didn't get the cane, yeah you can laugh, but I was a good boy. Peter was expelled from the school towards the end of its time at St Albans and he was eventually hanged for murder. Oh yes, he was hanged for murder. He divorced a girl he married from Mount Pleasant School and went off with another woman to South Africa, where he was convicted of her murder and two or three others. So whether the caning perhaps wasn't good enough I don't know, but he didn't get enough caning in my opinion, but then again perhaps it did the wrong thing, I don't know. He was a right 'tear away'.

Academically I found it quite good at St Albans and I eventually took the exams at the end. I remember we had to take London School Certificate in the right subjects; one had to be this and one that. There had to be a language. I remember the old French master telling me that was the one thing that was going to let me down but I got a credit, I think because he said I wouldn't get it; it made me try harder. So I got my Matric exemption. Yeah, but I couldn't go to University. The reasons for that were partly my upbringing, part of my background and part of the war I suppose, in a way. You see my mother had worked for me as I say from when I was three until I was fourteen, then she remarried when I was fourteen, so she'd had a hard time for those twelve or thirteen years and I felt I needed to earn money and not rely on her any more. Then, when I left school, we'd got conscription coming along, National Service, and I wanted to go into telephone engineering particularly, or radio engineering, something in that line. All of my school friends were going into banking and similar things but I didn't want to go into banking, that wasn't what I was looking for; I was looking for something mechanical or electro-mechanical.

I knew what I wanted to do, but because of the war I couldn't get into it. Everybody was coming home from the war, this was in 1945, and their jobs were being kept for them. So I couldn't get where I wanted and I finished up by going for an interview at the National Westminster Bank; they accepted me but I then got myself another job on a temporary basis, 'till I could get into radio engineering. I had to go to the Bank and tell them, the Bank Manager was nice about it. He was really nice about it because he said, if you don't like it, come back here and we've got an opening for you. Then of course a few weeks after that I had the chance to go in for a job that I wasn't really particularly interested in but it was a little more interesting I suppose, and that was Estate Agency and Auctioneering at Godfrey West and Hickmans, but had I gone there I would have been articled to them for three years., so I didn't go there either. Well, when they pointed out to me that I'd got to be with them for three years, articled to them for three years, it would have meant that I would have been twenty at the end. During those three years I'd have been on five shillings a week for the first year, ten shillings a week for the next year and fifteen shillings a week for the third year. They told me that they didn't take the five hundred pounds premium that they took before the war. But I worked it out that by that time I'd be twenty by then and I'd have to go into the army and do my two years National Service, which would make me twenty-two.

For that period of time I'd still be looking to my mother and what was then my stepfather to keep me, and I didn't think that that was right. So I stayed on the job I'd taken which lasted me until I came out of National Service but I didn't go back there. I knew I'd get a job where I really wanted to go, which was on Post Office Telephones which meant coming up to Medway Thames; that's how I came to this part of the country, I went into radio engineering for a little while, while I was waiting to come up here.

But going back to the evacuation, I left St Albans when I was sixteen, that's 1944,

Old Hastings Grammar School

yes, sixteen that's when I went back to Hastings but my mother hadn't gone back she was still in Taunton. By that time I'd got an aunt who was living in mother's house, she'd been there for a few months so I went back and stayed with her. I actually went back to school at Hastings back with the Grammar School to William Parker School. Oh, it was lovely; that school, it was old, not like St Albans School. I hadn't been there before but I'd walked past it when I was a little boy. We used to walk past when we went to the Alexandra Park; quite happily, every time my mum used to say, "That's where you're going to go one day." Then I didn't go there until I was sixteen but it was a nice school. Unfortunately the buildings have now gone, there are two houses there instead, they've demolished the whole school building and built the comprehensive in the old playing fields.

When eventually I went home I was more than happy, well how can I put it? I felt no different about it because soon after I was evacuated my mother was evacuated; she went to Taunton. My aunt and uncle were evacuated from Hastings to Taunton and eventually my mother went and lived with them down there. So, so far as Hastings was concerned, the only one that had been residing in our house at Hastings was the cat. My grandmother who lived opposite was going across every day and looking after him, he stayed there until the end of the war and we all went home.

Of course, with my mother in Taunton, I was going there from St Albans to see her for holidays, I wasn't going back to Hastings at all; so Hastings was somewhere different. My mother was in one place, I was in another place and there was nobody in actual fact in Hastings, except my grandparents. It was a complete disruption of our lives really and then of course while my mother was in Taunton, she married. I was fourteen and I knew my stepfather before she married him, I met him down there. It's a long story about how she met him, when she went down there she was working and it developed from there. She married him in 1943 when I was fourteen and a half, I felt all right about that yeah, quite happy, quite happy.

I was quite happy going back to Hastings itself even though my mother was at Taunton still and living with her father in law by the second marriage because her husband was away aircraft building at Bristol. But my aunt looked after me for a few months until my mother came back to Hastings and my stepfather followed her a month or two afterwards, and we all seemed to fit in all right. I could fit in with anybody after all the changes I'd had.

My mother didn't visit me at St Albans, it was always me going to Taunton and I've often said, I was only saying the other day, that when you think about it, at thirteen and fourteen I was travelling from St Albans to London and across London and down to Taunton. The first time I ever did it, I had an aunt who lived in London, who saw me across, but once I'd been shown how to use the Underground I did it myself. It wasn't as bad as it sounds because quite a few of the boys were going to their homes in Hastings and they found their way as well. We all used to go round the Circle Line dropping off at different stations you see. It was funny because coming back at the end of the school holidays we would meet each other on the same train. I never got caught in any of the raids in London. St Albans didn't get really badly hit; there was not a lot but we had a few doodlebugs and things, but mostly they didn't seem to reach that far; they were intended more for London I think. Hastings copped it. London obviously copped it. A number of times we used to go to school and at about the same time every day, we'd just about be walking past the air raid shelters and the sirens would go, so we dived in, straight into the same shelter, every day almost yeah.

I was very happy at Walkern. We went back there years ago, two or three years ago. When we came back from Derby, I said I'd like to call round to Walkern and have a look round, and I was amazed that it hasn't changed. The house was still there of course. Oh yeah, I wanted to go up to the door and knock but we went round the back; it was the Old Rectory and there was a lovely little lane that went up to the side by the church. The lane was a ford across the river and we went round there and parked the car round there. The tennis courts are not there now; there's a lawn. We used to go to church as a family basically, from the house. At St Albans it was a requirement at school that you went on church parade every Sunday morning. You were signed in to see that you were there; that was all right for me because I'd been in the choir at Hastings.

Going away gave me independence and I think, to be quite honest, it was good, the independence was good. Can I say it was good for everybody to become independent? In that way I think National Service was good for everybody because it gave them independence; but possibly from my point of view, it gave independence from a mother that I won't say doted on me or anything like that, but could have. I think she could have been I'm not saying 'dominant' but she could have been. It gave me a sort of break from a mother that would have had nobody else but me, I think it was good for both of us. I think it was extremely good for me that she married again during the war while she was away. I'm not going to say that I would have been one that was left looking after a mother for the rest of his days, but that is the sort of thing that can happen in cases like mine. If anyone else was in the same situation as mine, I think it would have been good for them. It was an intense relationship, being alone with her; it had to be of course, there was no way out of that. It was, you see the only family life that I'd had - me and me mum - that was about it, but there was my aunt and uncle who were almost mother and father to me at Hastings, particularly my uncle. Yeah, definitely, definitely he always was my father figure. He still was until he died . I'm not saying when mother remarried that L- was the one I didn't take any notice of; I respected him and I looked up to him and all the rest of it but of course, as a father figure, my uncle still took that place.
I think the war did me good. I hate to say the war was a good thing, I wouldn't say that, but what I would say is that good things do come out of it and as far as I'm concerned a lot of good came out of it. Quite honestly, I think the life I did have out of it has been good for me. Doreen was at the Central School (my first wife who died) but she went back to Hastings. I don't think they had the same education, I think they were farmed out to different schools, it was only a skeleton school, so I'm not quite sure what would have happened if I hadn't gone to the Grammar School, I've never thought of that.

I don't know why my mum went to Taunton. Mind you, I don't know what would have happened if she'd gone to where I was at St Albans. Where she would have lived I don't know, but she went to Bath with the next-door neighbours. Mum went there with them and eventually it wasn't long before she went to Taunton with her sister, my aunt and uncle. This was the aunt and uncle that almost had helped to bring me up, yeah. I was a bit marooned from them really but I used to go down for school holidays, you see, and I wrote letters.

If I look back on it generally, I think I could quite honestly say that the war did me no harm. In actual fact, as I say, it did me good. On the other hand, I mean you can never say what would happen if a situation hadn't happened. If the war hadn't happened, if I hadn't been evacuated, if my mother hadn't been evacuated, there's no way you could say what would have happened. I mean if I hadn't gone away, I would never have had such a broad outlook, because it broadened my outlook tremendously. It made me very, very, much more self-confident than ever I was before and of course, if my mother hadn't have been evacuated she would never have remarried. Well, she wouldn't have remarried the same chap and she might not have remarried at all. I don't know, but all I can say is that from what I can see came out of what happened, it wasn't a disaster. For me personally, no, it wasn't a disaster at all. It would have been different if somebody that you knew or loved had been killed in the war; obviously it puts an entirely different outlook on it altogether, and I'm not saying that the war was a wonderful thing or anything like that, far be it! I think it was horrible; but for me it was only good that came out of it in that respect. I think I got a good education as far as schooling was concerned. The only way that it was blighted was because of the situation I was put into whereby conscription followed on at the end of the war and interfered with my future, but that applied to all young men at the time.

During the actual school experience itself there was all this going from one place to another; we moved from building to building, transferred for different lessons. I mean we'd move in the middle of the morning to go to a different place, but it was just the way that it was. To be quite honest, the fact that I moved from one school to another school, it wasn't as if I'd known the second school any differently; if I'd moved from William Parker School building at Hastings I'd have compared it to that. I hadn't got that comparison but when I came back I loved it. Oh, I loved it and I think I would have compared it differently. Of course, the other thing was that a lot of the masters at the school had been taken away to serve in the Forces and we had got one or two that had come back that had really retired. I wouldn't say they were past it but they were definitely a little bit old in their ways, some of them. I still sing a little song from my Grammar School days that I remember.

We are the Hastings boys, far, far away.
We get bread and scrape, three times a day.
Eggs and bacon, we don't see.
We get sawdust in our tea,
That is why we're gradually...
Fading away... fading away....


## William Parker School Song

The corners of the earth have heard our footfalls,
On the seas of all the world our keels are known.
Lo! Now our name was made
Sport and study work and trade
'Ore ever James the first was on the throne.
No little thing our name and pride to carry,
Not small the weight of honour we sustain;
But it's up to us to bear it
'Till our younger brothers share it
To pass the school's tradition on again.

Refrain.
Brothers all, Hastonians, William Parker's sons.
We must guard the old renown, games or books or guns
Years ago and years ago bright the record came
In centuries that follow us bright it must remain.
Solo.
Hail the ancient brotherhood, let us bear the name.
Refrain.
Sons of WilliamParker.

We can do with jolly sportsmen for our fellows,
We can do with earnest scholars just the same,
But the bully and the sneak
And the slackey must not speak
 In the fellowship of us who play the game.
The pluck to lead that yet is proud in service,
Obedience to our ancient honoured rule,
And the faith that backs your friend
To the journey's utter end
Are the things that win your colours in the school.

159

Refrain
Brothers all...
Solo
What's the tie that makes you one, once again the name!
Refrain
Sons of William Parker.

(Basses) We have trodden in your pathways little brothers,
Our initials on your desk lids still remain.
We were proven by disaster
And we win to service vaster –
Stand to arms, the brave battalions of the slain.
Death for dower gave us power and great glory!
Yet at dusk we steal a moment to return
Do you feel our longing guide you?
Do you feel us sit beside you?
Does our whisper move your spirit as we yearn?
Refrain.
Brothers all...
Solo. In the hall a whisper, listen whence it came.
Refrain.
Sons of William Parker.

Oh The School's an older thing than any master!
And the School's a younger thing than any boy!
Though the years may carry on
'Till our company is gone
She stands beyond their power to destroy.
Her light has flamed through triumph and disaster;
Shall it shine a little brighter for your stay?
Stick it out the need is on you;
Days ahead depend upon you;
And the torch is in your keeping – light the way!
Refrain
Brothers all...
Solo
Fill your lungs with pride of it – brothers all – the name.

## The Grammar School at the Hastings White Rock Baths in 1945.

^

Terry between third and fourth from the right.

**Chapter 14. 'They had nailed down the coffin, no one could see him.'**

**Lillian's Story.**

My name is Lillian Wood; my name when I was born was Apps, and I have a sister Daphne who was evacuated with me. I come from the fishing community in Hastings. My paternal grandmother was the last one to hold an official licence for selling fish from a fish cart. She was allowed to sell fish as it was landed from her cart on the beach, she would row out to sea with her husband and auction the fish as they landed it. Her brother was gassed in the First World War and died of it later. My maternal grandmother had a fish barrow and would take the fish round the streets.

We lived in a cottage in All Saints Street in the Bourne, but the cottage was eventually demolished and our family was given a council house. There were a lot of us, I was the fifth one of eight children; I had an older sister, then there was a baby that died, two older brothers, then me; after me come two younger brothers and one younger sister. My father originally went to sea when he was fourteen and he was called up when war broke out; one of my brothers joined the Fleet Air Arm and my older sister went into the Land Army. Life at home before the war was strict, my father used naval rules because there were so many of us. We sat on a bench at the table and we had to ask to get down, but I had the place at the end, and if there was any trouble it was always me that landed on the floor. He kind of regimented us and if we went too far he'd give us a 'back hander' but mum was a softy she would only go as far as saying "I'm going to leave you for a soldier".

I passed the scholarship and was in my second year at the High School when war broke out. My mother took in three evacuees from London; it made little difference to us as our house was always full as my mother also took in Bed & Breakfast guests. We'd only had these evacuees a short while when I remember the building of walls and tank traps against invasion after Dunkirk, which brought on our own evacuation. Notice came round and father said, "Let them go". I was twelve at the time and Daphne was seven. My two younger brothers went with All Saints School to St Albans, Fred was nine and Dick was five, mother was left alone at home.

Of course I remember the train and feeling worried about my mother and 'full up', lonely, and saying to myself, "God, where are we going to finish up?" We were gathered together somewhere in Ware to be sorted out and wondering all the time what was going to happen. We were walked up Muswell Hill, it seemed such a long way, just walking and walking. I remember an alleyway and a pub and four of us were left. Someone said, "They'll take two in here". So then there was Daphne and me until they said, "We'll have these two", it was like a cattle market and we were the last two left.

It was a Mrs Raymond who took us in, and the first thing she did was to give us a hot bath. The table was set for tea and all I could think was, 'My mum should be doing our tea now'. My sister was sitting on someone's lap, I was far too old for that but I was silent and troubled and thinking to myself, "I'm not sure whether I'm going to like this." But Mrs Raymond turned out to be like my mum, she was good to us, she provided for us and we could go to school. Over the back was a large turkey farm and we could hear that noise all the time - 'gobble-gobble'.

Everything began to fall into place. There were three bedrooms in that house, the older son was in the army, we had his room and they had a daughter older than us, and a younger son. When the older one came home on leave the parents gave up their own bed for him, we were never turned out. My sister Daphne and I shared a bed. She wet the bed but my foster mother was good about it, she never punished her. I suppose she felt insecure because she had left my mum, but at the time I thought the reason was that the toilet was down the garden and you knew you needed to go but couldn't face the cold and would snuggle down and leave it until the last minute and then it was too late.

We went to Mrs Raymond's daughter's wedding; they bought a new dress for Daphne to go in but they didn't buy one for me. I don't remember my mother visiting us there but my older sister came and made me a dress. My attitude was to hold myself back for my own mum and thinking, "I'm not going to give all of me." My brothers weren't happy in St Albans and my father went down and took them home; then my mum took the boys and went to live with them in Somerset.

The schooling was very basic and there was some bombing; I didn't feel it was very safe in Ware. There was a cellar in my foster parents house and every time the siren went we all went down there. I missed my father too; he could do anything; even make and mend our shoes because he could sew leather together and when coats were handed down from our cousins he would unpick them, cut the pieces into the right size and sew them back together to fit on his machine, he was a great sewer. He was the one who always looked through our hair for lice or nits with a metal comb, and made sure we were all clean and warmly dressed.

At our foster home the son who was younger than us was a bit jealous of us, I suppose, and he complained about the food, - said we were having some of his sugar ration. So my foster mother, who was very fair, gave all of us children our own sugar ration in a jar, so we had to make it last. She treated us the same as her own children and on Saturday mornings we all went to the cinema together.

One Monday morning my father went to Somerset and collected mum and the boys and took them to the Isle of Man because he'd found a room there with more accommodation. He said we all had to be together, so we had to leave Ware. We went to see Miss DeGroochey, the Deputy Head but she said there was no High School in the Isle of Man to transfer us too. Anyway we felt we were wasting our time at Ware because the education was so basic, and my father gave us no choice at the time, to him the thing that mattered was that the family was back together, reunited. At Ware the fact that I had my sister helped to make it all right for me, - 'took off' the loneliness, so I understood what he meant.

When we got to the Isle of Man the local children took the pee out of us because of our accent and although my sister and I were always fighting and arguing we always stuck up for each other if someone else had a go. The accommodation was larger but we were still living in one big room and in March 1941 my parents managed to find a flat in Douglas. My mother was able to make our clothes there and we began to feel more 'up market' because we had good clothes and a good flat. Then my dad was transferred to Portsmouth, he was a Sub-Lieutenant by this time and he was so good looking. I was so proud of him and when he came to see us I would say to my friends, "That's my dad!" When he went to Portsmouth my mum went to see him off and on the way he called at Hastings to see the one older brother who had stayed there. Before he could embark on his ship, Portsmouth was bombed and he was killed before the ship left; there were twelve of them killed in the Officer's Mess on that day. A telegram was sent. My mother went down to see him but they wouldn't let her; they had nailed down the coffin, so no one could see him.

Mum reacted straight away by saying we had to go home as soon as she got back. There was a ferry next day from the island. She put all our things into carrier bags, those brown paper ones with string handles, we each had to carry our own. We stayed on the way in Liverpool or Birkenhead, I can't remember which, but I know it was Lime Street. My mother was possessed by a kind of nervous energy. She took us all on the train to London and then from London to Brighton but we were on the last train, there were no more trains that night, so we were all locked in the waiting room at Brighton station by the police, and we slept there that night.

By the time we got back to Hastings I was fourteen. There was no schooling so I went to work. I found a job during that March 1941 in a fashion house at seven and sixpence a week, then later on I found a better job in Boots and got married when I was nineteen.

Because of the war we lost a lot when my father died, we paid for it. My mother had us all to feed so she took in washing and did Bed & Breakfast with meals. We all had to give up our beds, if necessary, to the visitors but we always had the best of food. My father was forty-nine when he died, when they sealed his coffin we felt it had to be, it was just part of life but we hadn't prepared ourselves for his death because on the Isle of Man life seemed good. When dad joined the navy at fourteen he was a cabin boy, he had a hard life, they were still using rigging. His mother was a fisherwoman who went round selling fish in a basket and she was a hard woman who wanted her son to take care of her when he married, so he paid the Council two shillings and six pence a week to help her. My mother died in a nursing home, I worked there later after she died but I feel that things would have turned out better if it hadn't been for the war, the quality of life would have been different.

There was a lot of bombing in Hastings, one dropped on Keeves and a pub near us and Woolworths. During raids we all sheltered under the table in the kitchen, we never thought we would be killed in spite of what happened to my father. We were under there one day when this dark shadow passed over us and we said, "What was that?" It was a bomb that bounced, it went off nearby but if it hadn't bounced we would have been killed, it was very low, near our heads. Then there were the Doodlebugs, there was no siren to warn you but you would hear them come over and just had to wait for them to go off.

I have a son and a daughter, they are fine and my son got himself a degree. I used to say my father was the clever one but one day someone said, "You think it's your father, but there's nothing wrong with your mother's brain, she's a bright one," she never spelt anything wrong in her life. My older brothers and sister had all passed the scholarship and gone through the Grammar School and the High School. Education was not valued in those days and for us during the war it was less important than the family all sticking together. I never questioned it when I had to come home and give up my education. I still think it was important to come back home when my father died, to the community where people would all stick together, help one another out.

I'm an optimist but I still think the war did us a great deal of harm and changed our whole lives. I've never moved far from the community, I still go down there and still see a lot of my sister.

## Daphne's Story (Lillian's sister.)

My name is Daphne Mitchell. I was Daphne Apps when I was evacuated with my twelve year old sister Lillian and I was only five, the next to youngest in the family. I can't remember getting on to the train or saying goodbye, only looking out of the window and thinking we were going on an outing, it didn't seem like a trauma. I thought we were going to have a tea party but then I saw Lillian was crying. I asked her why she was crying but she said, "I'm not, I've got something in my eye," and I said, "No, you're crying".

I remember having a letter from my mum and being allowed to sit next to my sister at the High School until they found a school I could go to myself. This took about two months.

I was pretty 'street wise' even at five but the toilet was up the garden and I was too frightened to go up there in the night and I wet the bed but I don't remember being told off about this. Our foster parents were lovely. My foster father used to let me help him weigh potatoes in his shop and sort out vegetables and he made me a pram out of an onion box. I have a vivid memory of my foster mother walking me to the cemetery every Sunday, she always took me with her and held my hand; the thing I remember is her hand twitching as she held mine. Betty, her daughter played games with me. I can't remember saying goodbye to my foster mother when we left.

When we went off with my mum back to Hastings I can remember her crying but it didn't register that my dad had died, I didn't understand death at the time. When we got back some of my friends were still there, so I could go out to play with them. My older brother was more like a father but I remember wanting my dad to be there to take me for a walk on Sundays. The rationing never worried me, my mum made sure we didn't miss out; she would buy rations from other people.

By the time I was nine I was attending school either in the morning or afternoon, just half time but up until then there was no school or only one day a week; the only time I had full time schooling was for the last year before I left at fourteen. I attended Clive Vale School and did well. I was always top of the class with a girl called Sonia, but any exam. would always put me in a panic.

# Chapter 15. 'It was very much dominated by policy and procedure.'

## Tony Pelling's Story.

I was born in Silverhill in Silverlands Road in 1925. I've no brothers and sisters; I'm an only one. My father ran a Corn Merchants shop at Silverhill Junction. He'd been involved in the First World War; he was a

lorry driver in what I suppose you'd now call the RASC. I think it was the ASC in those days, it was the Army Service Corps then. He was involved in France in taking the ammunition to the notorious Hill 60. I think it was at the Somme, I know he was there throughout most of the war; he finished up with all the general service medals and that sort of thing.

At the outbreak of the Second World War he was running the business on his own. I'd attended Tower Road Junior mixed and Infants School from 1930 to 36, then I got a scholarship to the old Hastings Grammar School and had a very happy life at home in those days, with plenty of friends around of my own age. We were able to play in the street on our bikes, with hoops and marbles and all that kind of thing that we did when we were young, and Tower Road School was very good. When I got to the Grammar school, I was very happy and I did very well and managed to collect one or two prizes while I was there. What I disliked most at the Grammar school, I think, was physical exercise and also the class, which was described as manual, which is woodwork in these modern days. In all the other subjects apart from art, I did very well, so I suppose I was considered to be a good student. When the time came to be evacuated I was going to leave. The Headmaster spoke to my father and said it was a great pity I was going because he had hoped that I would be a State Scholar, which in those days was quite something. Obviously I had hoped to go to University, although there were no Careers Advisors and I hadn't much idea of what I might do. I had vague ideas about going to the London School of Economics or to Nottingham University, but of course that all disappeared with evacuation.

So I was evacuated in July, I remember the arrival in St Albans very well. My friend and I, we were two of the larger lads and our group had all been taken to the Hatfield Road Senior Boys School, where the would be foster parents came to collect the evacuees and the two of us, being rather large fellows got left behind. Nobody wanted us. Nobody wanted us, because we were obviously going to eat a lot. So the Billeting Officer sort of 'hawked' us round from place to place. She knocked on doors and couldn't find anybody to take us. She spotted a Special Constable and stopped the car and said "You wouldn't know anybody who would take these two fifteen year old boys in I suppose?" He said "Oh, I think my wife would be glad to take them in". So he turned around and went to Beech Road where they lived, which were very new semi-detached houses. He by trade was a building sub contractor, and they took us in. Of course I'd been an only child up to then and at this stage I had to share a bed with Alex my friend, which was unusual for me and for him as well, because he too was an only child.

They were very house-proud people and obviously it was very new. I think he may have been concerned with the building of it really as he was in the trade, and everything was so spotlessly clean that the sitting room was never used at all. It had been set out, just as it had been seen in the shop. The front hall was parquet flooring. We weren't allowed in the front door. You always had to go to the back and take your shoes off. They'd got a big Labrador dog called Moses. If people came to the door, which they normally did, he would rush to the door and skid along on the parquet floor. He was about the only one that was allowed along there, which was rather funny.

When we got to St Albans the air raids were beginning to take place. We were instructed that if there was an air raid alert when we were on the way to school, we had to knock on the door and find shelter until the all clear went, which naturally took up time and we had to do that quite often. We shared St Albans School, which was a semi-public school and found this rather strange because the prefects wore short gowns and carried canes so they could punish the younger ones, which we didn't do at the Grammar School. We weren't directly concerned with them because they met for half the day and then we shared the other half with them, which wasn't a very satisfactory arrangement of course. We had classes in a place called The Abbey Institute that had been a non-conformist church in Spicer Street, and we used to have a fair amount of homework to do, and then we had to go to church every Sunday. I was Church of England at the time, so that didn't come amiss, particularly because I'd been a churchgoer up to that point and been confirmed, so it wasn't strange.

At a slightly later stage my mother and her sister came to live in St Albans. We had friends who'd moved from Hastings to St Albans, sometime before the war. My aunt, who had come to live with us in Silverlands Road, had a nervous breakdown and as the war progressed my mother felt she should take her away from the South Coast and so they came to live with these friends of ours and I was able to visit them from time to time. I still lived with the foster parents and my father used to come up on Sundays in the Maidstone and District coach that brought parents to visit on. He would come with a friend of his. I don't know as it was much of a day out really because most times on the way back in the evenings they were involved in some sort of air raid in London. You had to go through London in those days; there was no M25 or anything like that.

The coaches came pretty regularly. I don't know whether they did something similar to other evacuees in other parts of Hertfordshire and Bedfordshire because of course the Hastings children were spread amongst various villages and towns in both counties. The High School was at Ware in Hertfordshire and the Hastings Central School was at Welwyn Garden City; so it was spread around pretty well. I got to know of course more about that after I came back and worked in the Education Office, and got involved then with the evacuated schools. I can't remember what my family's reasons were for coming back in November 1940 but things had eased off as far as bombing was concerned. We all came back, of course, to live in our house in Silverlands Road.

I could have stayed on but I didn't, so I must have felt that it was better to come back to Hastings at the time. I wasn't able to take my General Schools (as it was in those days) until after I'd left school a little later on when Evening Schools restarted about 1943–4 but I didn't use the Matric to get into University. The chances of getting in would have gone by then because of course I was liable to be called up by that time, which in the event I wasn't, so things went off in a different direction altogether.

A lot of contemporaries had returned at that stage and children from other evacuated areas had come back as well. There was a general drift back into Hastings. My father, of course, had got to carry on his business as

best he could and my mother, I suppose, felt she ought to be back with him. So I came back with them to help my father out in his shop because his employee had been called up, so he had no help. He'd got to do deliveries himself and needed somebody to look after the shop while he was out, but I had no schooling then for a year 1940-41, except that I was studying privately with Bennett College, a Correspondence College with a famous advertisement, 'Let me be your father'. Obviously this wasn't satisfactory for me as a long-term issue and my father knew that, so when a vacancy came up for a Junior Clerk in the Education Office in 1941, I applied with about ten others. We sat round and did an examination, in what was those days the Committee Room in Wellington Square and I was the fortunate one to be selected for the princely sum of forty pounds a year plus bonus.

There was a certain amount of bombing going on all the time in Hastings. It was described as Tip and Run raids. The German fighter-bombers used to rush in; they were after genuine targets like the station and gas works; so they would drop their bombs and be gone in next to no time. Eventually, of course, my father's shop in Silverhill was badly damaged on Thursday 11$^{th}$ March 1944; I remember it very well. I was working in the Education Office, based then in Hollington Park School, it was only a small office. There were about six of us and it was decided that we would also be the daytime Civil Defence Organisation and Control Centre. I was on duty at the time of that air raid. In fact the building we were in had cannon shells through the wall. It was such low level bombing that shots went straight through it but we stayed there until towards the end of the war. We were still there when the Flying Bombs were coming in 1944. I remember the bombing of Silverhill well because that particular Sunday we were working overtime, making arrangements for the second evacuation due to the arrival of the Flying Bombs. It was a bomb at Silverhill Junction that damaged my father's shop on 11$^{th}$ March 1944. About six of the shops were demolished, but his was the first one that wasn't completely, the windows and everything had gone out of it but it survived. My father carried on there until he died in 1955 but now it's all gone and it's a supermarket. It's quite different now to the Silverhill that was, the shops were pushed back to a different line. We were on Civil Defence Duty at the Control Centre that day and of course I knew the bomb had dropped at Silverhill. It was probably one of the biggest air raids that Hastings had experienced because it demolished St Matthews's church and damaged a Police Station in Battle Road and quite a few other places as well, and people were killed. My old education chief came down. He wasn't at Hollington Park office at the time because he didn't take part in the Civil Defence exercise. That was Mr W Norman King; he was appropriately named of course William Norman King of Hastings, which he was always very proud of.

He came down to the Control Centre; having walked to Silverhill about a couple of hours after the raid and said, "I think you ought to get back as soon as you can, as things are very dodgy in Silverhill Junction." By that time of course we'd done most of our duty by sending out rescue parties, ambulances and all that sort of thing. So I popped home which was only about five minutes on my bike, to see my dad sweeping his front window into the street and the rescue teams all working in Silverhill Junction to get out the one or two who survived and several who unfortunately didn't. They were all quite well known, all shopkeepers and their families around our way. That was 1944, quite late in the war. There had been bombing, of course, throughout the war and there were many very nasty incidents. The Albany Hotel was completely demolished when it was full of Canadian soldiers, and a lot of them were killed but there was never any publication of the numbers. They also dropped bombs on the troops and the Air Force using Marine Court, the skyscraper, as a base. They were marching one day at the back of Marine Court when a bomb dropped and a number of those were killed. I think perhaps the troops didn't get mentioned very much because there was never anything official said about it; it was hushed up. Marine Court itself had a gun on the end that faces towards Hastings, which pre-war I think was a Restaurant. This machine gun was used, of course, to good effect when the planes were doing Tip and Run because they were actually firing down on them as they went along the sea front.

There was considerable discussion at the Education Department about the children who were coming back from evacuation; they were in a cleft stick really and basically in charge of their return. Some children had come back of their own accord, but they weren't having any sort of education. They'd got to do something, so they opened a number of emergency schools; there was one in Ore and one in Hollington but some of the school buildings, of course, were not available because they had been bombed, like Sandown, Tower Road and St Andrews and some had been used for storing furniture, like Mount Pleasant which was full of furniture from people's bombed-out houses, and the High School was used as a store for coffins; so regard had to be given to the school buildings that weren't there any more, or needed for other purposes. This is why they had to set up emergency schools, but eventually they expanded to the point where some schools could came back because it was possible to be normal.

Then followed the flying bombs. They started coming on 6th June 1944 and because of that there was a second evacuation, which was arranged for people who wanted to send their children away again to Merthyr Tydfil in this case. That was just anybody, they didn't go as a school, they just went as a Hastings contingent; it was rather appropriately led by a Mr Evans, who'd been Headmaster of St Edmonds Central School, he took the children off to Wales, - well those who wanted to go. I'm not sure how many went now, but I think it was a trainload.

Of course, towards the end of the war everybody came back, but I don't remember any official date of return. I don't remember collecting up children from the various parts of Bedfordshire and Hertfordshire and so on, they must have just drifted back again. Then of course there were children who'd gone with their parents individually to Somerset and Cornwall; mainly, I think, parents with very young children under school age who went down to various West Country places when they had had the opportunity, and were very scattered.

The Welsh scheme was successful, I think, because it got rid of, if one could put it that way, quite a number of children from the area. We were fortunate that no flying bombs fell on any schools that still existed in those days; most of them went over the top and were brought down on the outskirts, out in the country of course. We used to chase them with Spitfires, which manoeuvred to tip them up. It was a sight to see a plane going alongside a doodlebug and going 'flip,' and the doodlebug would go down and crash somewhere out in the rural area where hopefully it was fairly safe. I could see that from where our office was, just behind the park. We were still available for duty in the Civil Defence Control Centre and stayed there and working until the end of the war, sending ambulances and rescue teams. We were the Control Centre; the co-ordinating centre, operating in the basement at Hollington Park; which had to be structurally reinforced. We had this huge map and various people marked where the bombs had fallen, and also placed pins for some service that had been sent, whether it was the Fire Brigade or the ambulance or whatever and what the strength was. They knew who had gone where, and where they'd still got available equipment if something else happened whilst they were out. It's quite a complicated business and of course at times when the bombing got bad, they brought in rescue parties from elsewhere. There was a National Organisation of Air Raid Precaution squads, at least two of them at one stage were based at Hollington Park because, being an old residential school for girls, there were plenty of bedrooms and things to house men who were brought in for this sort of thing. Quite apart from that, the night duty squad for the Civil Defence Control Centre staff slept in the building. Then if anything happened the alarm went, and downstairs they went to carry out their duties.

Going back to the return of the evacuees, that was quite haphazard really, apart from the lack of availability of the buildings there were also staffing problems. A lot of the staff had been sent to the evacuation areas, so they weren't all readily available to be reused. To open schools back here they had to get them equipped and then staffed, bring some of the Hastings teaching staff back. Somebody had to decide where the numbers in the evacuation area justified pulling staff out to bring them back here. They staggered it; they sort of picked them out one at a time. Obviously they started off by picking the old Head Teacher to start a school going, then picked staff from all over the place to start up these emergency schools. Ore, Silverdale, gradually built up to get back to pre-war conditions as far as possible, but then of course they were very short of schools by then, because they had been bombed. The 1944 Education Act had come in and the Development Plan had to be attended to, which meant new schools had to be built because between the wars there was only one new school in Hastings and that was Red Lake, with Robert Mitchell Special School for physically handicapped children attached to it. Apart from that, all the old schools were 1800s or 1900s and could do with replacing, quite apart from the loss of school buildings by war damage.
The Education Department was mainly responsible for schools going away. I imagine that the Hastings Evacuation Office kept a record of actually who went on the official evacuation, the main one that we were concerned with, and later on the one to Wales, and the people who went officially to Somerset and Cornwall. But other people who just drifted away of their own accord, of course there will be no record of those; nobody knows where they went, they might have gone anywhere. It could have been East Anglia, Yorkshire or any part of the globe.
But the Education Department's policy with regard to evacuees returning with their schools was the need of school buildings to come back to, and teachers to teach in them and all that sort of thing. There was correspondence between the Hastings authority and the Bedfordshire and the Hertfordshire authorities in those days because I imagine at that time that at some of the smaller village schools, the Hastings staff was

integrated with the staff of schools where they went, and to pull them out could create difficulties in the evacuation area. At the same time there were teachers being called up for military service, so if a man teacher evacuated with his school and then got his call up papers, he was lost to us. We were still paying the salaries of the teachers from this area; Hastings paid the Hastings' teachers, in the same way that we paid teachers who were on war service a supplement, depending on what they had. It became rather complicated of course; we had to find out what the teachers were earning in the forces; some of the teachers were humble privates, whilst others rose to Squadron Leaders. Their pension had to be retained and a certain amount paid for their pension and a certain amount by way of salary. It became very complicated when staff got sent, say, to the Far East and you didn't hear from them for months and months or even years, whether they were dead or alive, or what their pay was. When they came back there had to be a glorious reconciliation statement of what their service pay was, or what we owed them, or what they owed us even.

Another area of work was, of course, maintenance grants for children in the Grammar School and High School, and uniform grants depending on means tests for scholarship children, such as I had. They were technically free places, but if the parents earned enough, they would be asked to make a contribution towards the education fees. Then of course from 1944 all education was free, and so anybody who had been paying fees didn't pay any more if they were at a state school. We had an awful lot to deal with in a way, which the war complicated greatly. I imagine that quite a lot of pupils perhaps stayed away, where they'd been sent. Evacuation wasn't compulsory, there were lots of inducements to go, but you didn't have to go. As I said just now, when the older people left school in the reception area they got jobs and stayed there, because in the sort of areas we are talking about there were so many aircraft factories for example that must have provided work. It well could have happened to me if I'd stayed on. And then of course as time went on, people got called up and didn't come back for quite a while, and then conscription continued after the war.

For me it was both a personal and official experience really. As far as I personally was concerned, it obviously made a difference to me. If I'd stayed at school and the school had stayed in Hastings I would probably have gone to University: done something different to what I ultimately did. I suppose at one stage I did have regrets about it, when perhaps some of my contemporaries stayed the course and got on to University, although fewer people went to University in those days.

I actually got Matriculation. You couldn't take the General Schools as a non-school pupil; the only thing you could take was Matric. Whereas with the General Schools, you were given Matriculation Exemption if you got five pass subjects. I got my Matric but didn't do any more with it, its real purpose was University entrance. It was useful to say that I had got it. But I think the Headmaster of the Grammar School said on one occasion in a pre-war Speech Day that he wished employers wouldn't insist on school leavers having Matriculation, because Matriculation was intended solely for University, not for going into industry and commerce. So, yes, the war and evacuation did blight my career possibilities; and then there was the question of whether I was going to be called up or not; that hung over me. When I was seventeen I was looking for another job and rather fancied going into Banking, I don't know why, must have been mad I think. I went for an interview to five or six Banks and they all said, "Very sorry, but you are too old, you are going to be called up next year". But as it happened I wasn't. When I was rejected for the services, the understanding was that I stayed doing the job that I was doing, the sort of job that was reasonably essential I suppose; so they didn't put me into agriculture or something else, I stayed on at the Education Office. Well, it was the hub of the local education system, such as it was, and of course it was an interesting time with the '44 Act coming in and it was then built up from there.

To go back to evacuation, I suppose it was a good thing. It will never be quite known how many lives it saved but our evacuation, - the Hastings evacuation - was to get away from the possibility of invasion, which didn't take place. The London evacuation when they came here was obviously against the possibility of bombing, which did in fact take place. The bombing did to some extent take place in Hastings as well. We didn't have enormous night raids and day raids like they did in the East End and other places like Bristol and Bath; but the threat of invasion was there until the tide had turned, and we were sort of looking at invading Europe instead. There was always the possibility that there might be some sort of invasion. The pillboxes, the tank traps - conical things they dotted about all over the place - and they put mines here there and everywhere. You couldn't get in and out of Hastings without permission; it was a defence area; the whole thing was like a military operation. If you went out past the Ridge, when you came back through Harrow Arch there was a soldier saying, "Where are you going and why?" You had to produce your identity card before they let you in.

For younger children evacuation must have been quite terrible, because they would have felt they'd really been wrenched away from their parents and didn't know whether they'd ever see them again. I suppose there was that feeling in their selves as time went by and they heard about bombings and wondered what was happening at home because of course, there wasn't detailed news. They didn't say, you know, "The bomb has dropped in Silverhill" or something but "Bombs were dropped on the South Coast." It could have been anywhere, so there was always the thought, "was it somewhere you knew, or on somebody that you knew?" I was worried about my own parents and missed them. I'd never left home to any extent at that stage; I'd never been very far. I think we've got to bear in mind that we didn't have cars and go spinning about. I think the furthest I had ever been was to London once or twice. I'd been to Portsmouth on a school outing but I'd never been further than that. So to go to St Albans, which was North of London, was almost like going to a foreign country. It was without knowing where you were going as well, so that was fairly traumatic, and I suppose at the time being hawked around to find a billet, which was a bit traumatic as well. Here was everybody else being taken off! Not a very nice feeling to be the two left behind; to be the little boy that Santa Claus forgot. I can laugh now, but it was a chancy meeting, seeing this chap on his bike; or otherwise I suppose the Billeting Officer would have gone on going around from door to door.

I remember that until we met Mr H-, the billeting officer had taken us to one or two places and we'd never even got out of the car. She'd said, "I don't think this is a suitable place for you". At least they were pretty selective in where they were trying to put us I suppose. So we finished up with Mr and Mrs H- at 'Beetstan'. She was called Beatrice and he was called Stanley, hence the name of the house; and I kept in touch with them after the war. In fact I cycled to St Albans once with a friend and went to visit them.

I didn't fall out with them, although there was a bit of a problem. They weren't used to children at all, they'd never had any. I suppose they treated us as adults really. They weren't used to boys going to school and bags and bringing home homework. As an only child it was a bit of a wrench to leave my parents and live with another boy, - also an only child - and be expected to share my bed with him. He obviously found the same because he was in the same situation as myself, except that he'd got no father anyway; his mother was a widow. He eventually left and went to another billet at Harpenden Road but he came back to Hastings much about the same time as I did. We met fairly frequently after he was back in Hastings

It was a relief to be back home, although of course, as I say, we were subject to bombing. There were one or two people who set up as private tutors. Some friends of mine went to a chap called Rev Ray Godfrey, he lived at Markwick Terrace and took private pupils. I didn't go to him in the end because I did some of this correspondence course. Later on as schools reopened, evening classes started, so I went to Tower Road Infants School and finished off. It wasn't easy. It was helpful to carry on with textbooks at my own pace and that sort of thing, but it was far from ideal.

Going back to my billet, I think we were fed all right and it was clean, very clean. But I suppose the chap we were staying with Mr H-, I don't know how to put this really; but he wasn't a particularly well-educated fellow. Perhaps we weren't on quite the same wavelength as I might have been when I was at home. My dad couldn't claim to be very well educated, but the conversation might have been a bit different at home. He was always out, my foster parent; he was always out working because he was sub contracting on these aircraft factories, you see. We didn't see an enormous amount of him. It was a bit lonely. There was no great social life going on at the school, not as there had been when the school was here. The scouts continued but I didn't belong to the scouts. When Mr H- said to the Billeting Officer, "Well, come and see my wife and I'm sure she will take them in." She obviously hadn't been mad keen to take evacuees, otherwise she would have been already satisfied. Yes, I suppose that was the problem, not being in our own home as it were, we couldn't manage things in quite the same way

I think it was helpful with my work on evacuation to have been on the receiving end, but I don't know that it had much effect on what was done. It was very much dominated by policy and procedure, but at least you had some idea of what these folk were going through, 'putting up with', I think is the expression. The fact that I may have been deprived of a different future I think was the war in general, I don't think it was evacuation in particular. But the war itself meant that I didn't do what I had at an earlier stage hoped to do.

Now we've got two boys who both in fact went to University, Aston and Nottingham. My son loves Nottingham, feels it is the centre of England, there's a lot going on there. But we bought this house half a mile from Silverhill, my father always used to refer to it as the village. Someone who was here this morning said, "I'm just going up to the village". That's how I feel about it as well. It's my village, my home; I suppose we became part of Silverhill. This is where I belong.

**Tony as a young man.**

Hastings High School for Girls in 1939.

Some of the destruction of Hastings in October 1940

St. George's Road, Hastings, October 12, 1940

Left : Another view of the Bedford ruins.  Right : Wellington Road suffered i
same raid—October 5, 1940

Debris of Baptist Mission Hall, Priory Road, October 26

Front and rear of Havelock Road offices wrecked on October 8

**Pictures of air raid damage during 1940** copied from *Hastings &St.Leonards in the Front Line* 1985 2nd. Edition published by the Hastings & St. Leonards Observer newspaper.  First Edition published in 1945 by F J Parsons for the Observer.  Copy of the book held in the reference library at Hastings.

## On VJ Night

On VJ night we danced with delight
on the greensward next the sea.
Until I saw on the long wave races
riding the foam were young men's faces
with ghastly eyes watching me.
And it seemed as if from the grass blood rose
making me trip and stub my toes.

So I went to the edge of the victory prance
and sat alone in a state of trance.
Too many gone who were there before,
who could not cheer at the end of war.
And what have we done to the Land of the Sun?
How many Japanese slanting eyes
have we mushroomed to angels above the skies?
What have we done? What have we done?

"We've won! We've won! That's what we've done!"
you said as you came to me.
You lifted me up and kissed my ear
so I could not hear their voices.
Brushing away the tear on my cheek
you led me back to that frenzied joy;
my sweetheart, just sixteen, my boy.
You held me close, I felt your life -
it helped me forget about the strife.

I knew then that one day you or another
would plant a seed that I should mother.
A seed well nourished by soil made rich
from blood that ran in the field and ditch.
For life must spring from this death and fear.
Pray God the beginning of wisdom is here.

Sheila Rowe